CONTENTS

The Coming of the Civil War 1603–49

David Sharp

Series Editors
Martin Collier
Erica Lewis
Rosemary Rees

HEINEMANN ADVANCED HISTORY

Heinemann Educational Publishers
Halley Court, Jordan Hill, Oxford, OX2 8EJ
a division of Reed Educational & Professional Publishing Ltd
Heinemann is a registered trademark of Reed Educational & Professional Publishing Ltd

OXFORD MELBOURNE AUCKLAND
JOHANNESBURG BLANTYRE GABORONE
IBADAN PORTSMOUTH NH (USA) CHICAGO

First published 2000

ISBN 0 435 32713 5
02 01 00
10 9 8 7 6 5 4 3 2 1

Designed and typeset by Wyvern 21 Ltd

Printed and bound in Great Britain by The Bath Press Ltd, Bath

Picture research by Helen Reilly

Photographic acknowledgements
The authors and publisher would like to thank the following for permission to reproduce photographs: AKG London, p. 55; Bridgeman Art Library, pp. 26, 83, 87, 98, 106, 110; British Library, p. 45; Corbis, p. 58; Courtauld Institute of Art, p. 84; Fotomas Archive, pp. 38, 62; His Grace the Duke of Norfolk/Arundel Castle, p. 93; Mary Evans Picture Library, pp. 7, 17(r), 24, 36, 40, 46, 51, 73, 80, 88, 100; National Portrait Gallery, pp. 50, 115; National Trust Photographic Library, pp. 8, 11; Pat Hodgson Library, p. 17(l); Peter Newark Pictures, p. 121; Scottish Portrait Gallery/Earl of Roseby, p. 133; Victoria and Albert Museum, p. 32

Cover photograph: © AKG Photo London

HOW TO USE THIS BOOK

This book is intended for the AS examination. Its content covers the AS units for the following:

Edexcel

Unit 2. Personal rule and the crisis of monarchy in Britain 1629–42
Unit 3A. Crown, Parliament and conflict in early Stuart England 1603–29.

AQA

Option O

OCR

Unit 1. The English Civil War 1637–49
Unit 3. England 1603–40

Students should read through the relevant chapters and attempt the summary questions at the end of each chapter. Their aim is to challenge the reader to prioritise, analyse and explain the main concepts and events of the period. It is hoped that by doing this, students will gain a clearer understanding of the key features of each topic.

There is an assessment section at the back of the book. The questions have been modelled on the style of questions being used by the examination boards. There is guidance in the assessment section on how students might answer the questions.

INTRODUCTION

The period 1603–49 has attracted a lot of historical argument, and has probably been the subject of more books than any other period in English history. This is because, by the summer of 1642, England was locked into a bloody civil war that was to last until 1646, to be followed by another brief war in 1648. In 1649 Charles I was tried and executed in a revolutionary way, and England became a republic. Such dramatic events have naturally attracted much historical interest.

Some historians have looked for long-term causes for the Civil War, while others have argued that the events of the 1640s did not have any deep-rooted long-term origins.

James I (and VI of Scotland), King of England 1603–25, faced some problems during his reign. These problems centred round what sort of Church the Church of England should be, relations with his Parliaments, and royal finance.

Other than finance, James dealt reasonably well with these problems and, despite clashes with Parliament, he was never faced with a real challenge to his authority.

His son Charles, who succeeded him in 1625, soon found himself in strong disagreements with many of his subjects. By 1629 he had decided to rule without Parliament and had no plans to call Parliament again. His 'Personal Rule' from 1629 to 1640 was viewed with distrust by many people, as he not only seemed to wish to rule as an absolute monarch, but also his policies in finance, religion and foreign policy were directly contrary to the beliefs and attitudes of his subjects. In 1637 he was faced with a revolt in his Scottish kingdom and the English gave him very little support. He had to call Parliament in 1640 as he had no money left to fight the Scots.

Between 1640 and 1642 Charles failed to come to an understanding with Parliament, which was deeply suspicious of his advisers and thought he had a 'hidden agenda'. In November 1641 rebellion broke out in Ireland, but because of MPs' continuing distrust of Charles, they refused to pay for an army to put down the rebellion if Charles was to be in control of that army. MPs thought that if Charles had control of an army he might use it, not against Irish rebels, but to establish a royal dictatorship in England. However, it had always been the legal right of the monarch to command the army, and Charles was not going to give this up. Civil war was the result – a war that tore much of England apart.

After Charles' defeat in 1646, there was still no settlement because Charles still believed he could get all his powers back, if he 'strung out' negotiations long enough. However, more extreme groups, especially in the Parliamentary army, began to think in terms of deposing Charles. When Charles started the Second Civil War, their anger with him made them determined to execute him. These 'radicals' had power because of their influence in the army, although they were a minority in Parliament. The army 'purged' Parliament of MPs who were not prepared to try the king as a war criminal.

The king was put on trial, but he refused to answer the charges because he argued that no one could try the king. He was found guilty and executed on 30 January 1649.

FURTHER READING

A vast number of books have been written about this period. Below are some suggestions for further reading.

Martyn Bennett, *The Civil Wars 1637–53*
Barry Coward, *The Stuart Age*
Christopher Daniels and John Morrill, *Charles I*
Derek Hirst, *Authority and Conflict 1603–58*
John Kenyon, *The Stuarts*
Roger Lockyer, *The Early Stuarts 1603–42*

More challenging than these, for those who wish to go deeper into the ideas and arguments, are the following:

Robert Ashton, *Conservatism and Revolution 1603–49*
R. Cust (ed.), *The English Civil War*
A. Fletcher, *The Outbreak of the English Civil War*
Christopher Hill, *The Century of Revolution*
A. Hughes, *The Causes of the Civil War*
John Morrill, *The Revolt of the Provinces*
John Morrill, *Reactions to the English Civil War*
Conrad Russell, *The Causes of the English Civil War*
Conrad Russell, *The Fall of the British Monarchies 1632–42*

This period has been the subject of intensive debate amongst historians for many years and the above books are just a few of the many that have dealt with this period. Some historians have seen the Civil War as having long-term causes; others disagree, seeing there were no serious problems until 1637. The importance of events in Scotland and Ireland in causing the crisis of 1637–42 has been emphasised by some. This book can offer only an introduction to the period for the AS examination.

CHAPTER 1

Introduction

SOCIETY IN THE SEVENTEENTH CENTURY

Population

The population of England and Wales was approximately five and a half million in 1600. It had been rising steadily throughout the sixteenth century as the population became increasingly resistant to the recurring attacks of plague that had halved the population between 1349 and 1480. The vast majority of the population lived in the countryside, the poorest probably never travelling outside their village. There were cities, the major cities being Norwich, Bristol, York and Newcastle and one city that was huge by European standards – London. Already London was growing at a rate that dwarfed the other cities. In 1600 London's population was 250,000; by 1640 it was 400,000 – the largest city in Europe. The next largest city in England, Norwich, only had a population of perhaps 20,000. The size and wealth of London became a matter of envy and concern to the merchants of the 'outports' such as Hull and Lynn, who saw the great city, with its immensely rich **companies of merchants**, 'eating up the trade of the whole kingdom'.

KEY TERM

The merchant companies of London Trade to various parts of the known world was largely in the hands of the great city companies, who had royal charters (documents of rights granted by the king) to trade to various areas. The major companies were: the Merchant Adventurers trading to northern Europe, the Levant Company to Turkey, the Eastland Company to the Baltic, the Russia Company to Russia, and the East India Company to the Far East and India. The charters these companies had gave them a monopoly of trade. Merchants who were not members of these companies could not trade in these areas. Of course, merchants who were not members of the great chartered companies resented their hold on trade.

Life expectancy

Life expectancy was low for the vast majority of the population – those just 'making a living' as farm labourers or 'cottagers' (smallholders), for whom the average age of death was thirty. As child deaths were very high indeed, this figure gives a rather distorted view. In fact anyone who survived until fourteen had a chance of living until forty. For the more wealthy, with a better diet and rather better hygiene, life expectancy was higher. However, medical knowledge was, by our standards, all but non-existent. Death was a constant presence in every family; childbirth was particularly dangerous so children and wives were very much at risk.

Agriculture

For the majority of the population living in the countryside, life was bound up with the seasons and they lived by agriculture. Even England's main export, cloth, was based on the grazing of sheep. Poor weather in the summer months could mean starvation for many because, if the harvest failed, they were at risk in the following winter. However, in the seventeenth century demand for agricultural produce increased. The reason for this was the growth in population explained above. The growing cities needed to be fed and money was invested in improving river transport. The result was that landowners could get their goods to market more easily and were therefore encouraged to invest in agricultural improvements. Investment in agriculture and the increase in profits led to an increase in the number of large farms. Smaller farms were joined together to form farms of over 600 acres in size.

Industry

For centuries wool had been England's main export. By the seventeenth century England was not exporting much raw wool, but cloth that was 'unfinished'; it still needed to be dyed and 'dressed' – finished – to be made into clothes. This finishing was done in the Netherlands. New lightweight cloths that were suitable for warmer climates were also being developed. Although England exported some other goods, such as tin and leather, cloth remained the single most important export, with thousands of people, from shepherds, farmers, weavers and cloth buyers through to merchants, depending on it.

However, the cloth industry, like other sectors of the English economy, faced real problems at the beginning of the seventeenth century.

- **The guild system.** Industrial production was held back by the guild system. Guilds were organisations that made the rules for each trade, whether it be weaving, spinning or plumbing. The main effect of the guild system was to restrict those making specific goods so as to keep the price of those goods high. However, the result of this guild system was that it restricted output.

- **Poor communication and transport.** Although some rivers, including the Ouse, Nene and Thames, were made navigable in parts during the seventeenth century, it still took a long time to get goods to market. Most roads were tracks that became almost impassable in wet weather and harsh winters.

Social class

Social class in seventeenth-century England was very much more clearly defined and separated than today. In theory society was still hierarchical.

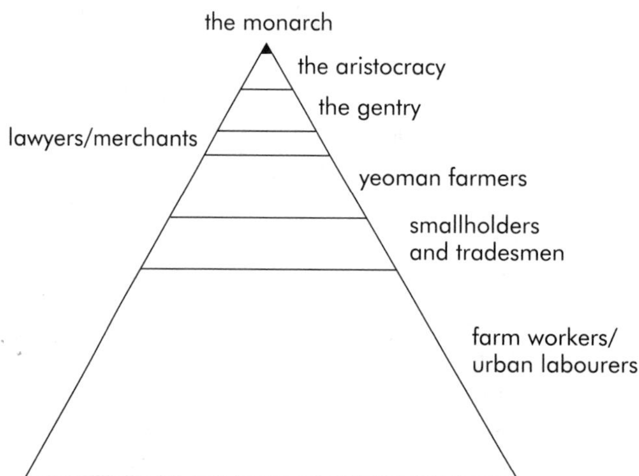

Aristocracy. The most important group in seventeenth-century society was the aristocracy – those with large estates whose families could, in most cases, be traced back for hundreds of years. They had inherited titles – Earl, Duke, Lord, Baron – which usually passed down to the eldest son. The eldest member of an aristocratic family sat in the House of Lords. Traditionally they had commanded armies, attended court and advised kings, and they arranged marriages among themselves – unless the family was going through a bad time financially, when they might arrange a marriage with the daughter of a rich merchant. They lived in the great houses that one can still see across England – Hardwick, Hatfield, Burleigh, Haddon, Knole, Holdenby – and they were surrounded by servants who 'lived in', some great houses having as many as fifty living-in servants.

Hatfield House, built by Robert Cecil, Earl of Salisbury.

Knights were a special case. Unlike the aristocracy with their hereditary titles, they were given their title of Sir by the monarch, usually for distinguished service or bravery, and the title did not pass down to the next generation. Those who held this title were very proud of it because it marked them off from the rest of the population.

Gentry. Below the aristocracy were the gentry – 'gentlemen'. The gentry are less easy to define. In theory, they had to be of 'old families' which did not have a hereditary title of honour, and they had a coat of arms, which showed that their family was 'old'. The gentry varied in wealth. Some could rival their local aristocrats in the number of acres they owned; others were considerably less wealthy. The gentry in the prosperous agricultural areas, such as the south, the midlands and East Anglia, were far richer than the gentry of the less prosperous north and west. The mark of the gentry family was that it did no work; like the aristocracy they let their land out to tenant farmers or had an 'estate manager' who organised the farms. Like the aristocracy, they were anxious to keep their landholding intact, so only the eldest son inherited the land; younger sons became lawyers or merchants. The gentry were vital to the running of the country outside London.

They served as **Justices of the Peace** and sheriffs. The leading gentry in each county got their status from being militia officers, Justices of the Peace, Deputy Lieutenants

KEY TERM

Justices of the Peace (JPs) were the unpaid administrators of the countryside. They undertook many of the following tasks:

- carrying out the instructions of the Royal Council
- trying criminal cases
- keeping law and order

Felbrigg, Norfolk, 1620.

(the organisers of the militia) and, the highest honour of all, Members of Parliament.

The militia was the only military force in England – except for a few garrisons at key points such as Portsmouth and Dover, and the Royal Guards around the court. There were very few professional soldiers in England. In theory, every man could be called upon by the monarch to help defend the country in time of war. Not everyone could be equipped and trained, even on a once-a-year meeting (muster). Therefore only some people were in the militia companies that were organised by each county. The Deputy Lieutenants were in charge of the militia in the counties, and the other leading gentlemen of each county were captains in charge of local companies. The weapons and gunpowder were often stored in the local parish church. Most militia companies were not at all well trained or equipped.

Lawyers and merchants. The lawyers and merchants were, in theory, below the gentry in terms of social status, although some were the younger sons of gentry. In fact, many lawyers and merchants were as rich as the leading gentry, or even aristocrats, and married into gentry or aristocratic families. Some of the great City of London merchants acted as moneylenders to both the aristocracy and gentry.

Yeomen. Next down the social scale were the yeoman farmers. These owned their own land, or rented large chunks of land from aristocracy or gentry. They did not claim to be 'gentlemen' and they worked their farms directly. Some successful yeomen, because they were hard-headed 'business farmers', were as rich as the gentry, but most were not. Yeoman farmers had done well in the later Elizabethan period and were to continue to prosper; some moved up into the gentry. Below the yeoman farmers were the 'cottagers' – those who had a few acres of land and also worked for yeoman farmers or the gentry.

The yeoman farmers seem to have done well between 1540 and 1640. They did not have the expenses of the aristocracy and gentry since they did not have to keep up a grand 'lifestyle' to impress others. The one expense they did take on was the rebuilding, improvement and extension of their houses. Many large farmhouses in England date from this period, known as the 'Great Rebuilding', and show how prosperous the yeomen were.

A yeoman's farmhouse at Bishopstone, Wiltshire, built in 1637.

The poor. The vast majority of the population were the rural poor – rural labourers who perhaps just had a cottage garden, or the urban workers in industries such as glass making, leather tanning and pottery. Some of these, if they were skilled workers, were in demand and could live quite well; others lived 'from hand to mouth'. There were specialised trades in the countryside, such as blacksmithing and weaving, but the latter was dependent on economic conditions. Occasionally economic depression caused widespread distress. In the 1620s and again in 1640 the wool trade was affected by recession and the weavers suffered.

The role of women

Seventeenth-century society was dominated by males. In theory, the head of the family exercised complete power over his children, and, by today's standards, women appear to have been oppressed. Legally, women were second-class citizens.

- Women could not, in theory, own or inherit land and most marriages among the upper classes – aristocracy, gentry and merchants – were arranged.
- Women could not vote and were regarded as inferior to men in every respect.

In practice, some women overcame these legal handicaps and exercised considerable influence. Despite the convention of arranged marriage, in the late sixteenth century, women such as Bess of Hardwick were able to make their 'own luck' by marrying the men they wished to, holding property and, through their forceful personalities, having real power. One of the most common themes in early-seventeenth-century plays is the daughter who defies her parents and marries for love. Moreover, the diaries of some seventeenth-century gentry and yeomen show that their wives had considerable power in the home and were able to exert influence over their husbands. During the Civil War, some women played an active role commanding troops defending their castles while their husbands were away fighting. Even the poorer women played an important role in the economic life of the country, particularly in the weaving industry – 40 per cent

A seventeenth-century family: the Spencers at Charlecote Park.

of weaving was done by women. However, in general it would be true to say that women were regarded as inferior and the 'weaker vessel'.

THE STRUCTURE OF POLITICS

The Crown

At the head of the political system was the monarch, with far greater powers than kings or queens have today.

The divine right of kings. There were many important ideas associated with the monarchy, the most significant being the 'divine right of kings'. During the sixteenth century ideas that had been around for several hundred years became more clearly expressed. The divine right of kings was an idea that appealed to monarchs all over Europe – monarchs who wished to extend their authority. In simple terms, the idea was this:

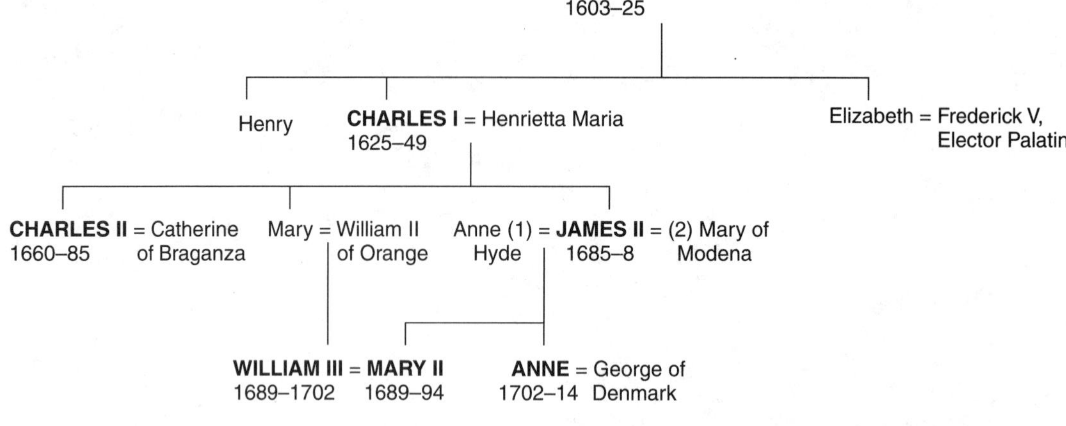

Part of the Stuart family tree. Monarchs are shown in bold capitals and the dates indicate their reigns.

- **Kings were God's representatives on earth.** Their power came from God and therefore could not be challenged.
- **God's will.** Those who believed in the divine right of kings believed that kings were carrying out God's will on earth, so again their decision could not be challenged.

The difference between Charles and James. Both James I and Charles I were, like all seventeenth-century monarchs, believers in the divine right. This belief is important because it helps to explain many of their decisions and actions. However, there was a difference between the two. Although James believed that he had been chosen by God to be king, he did not challenge the laws of the land or Parliament with this idea in mind. Charles was not so careful.

The royal prerogative. In English political theory, the king ruled as well as reigned. In other words, he had wide powers that could not, or should not, be challenged. Although the king had these powers, it did not mean that many people believed in the divine right of kings. The wide-ranging rights and powers that the monarch held were known as the 'royal prerogative'. The prerogative included the right:

- to give out titles of honour,
- to choose the Royal Council (the king's advisers),
- to conduct foreign policy,
- to appoint judges,

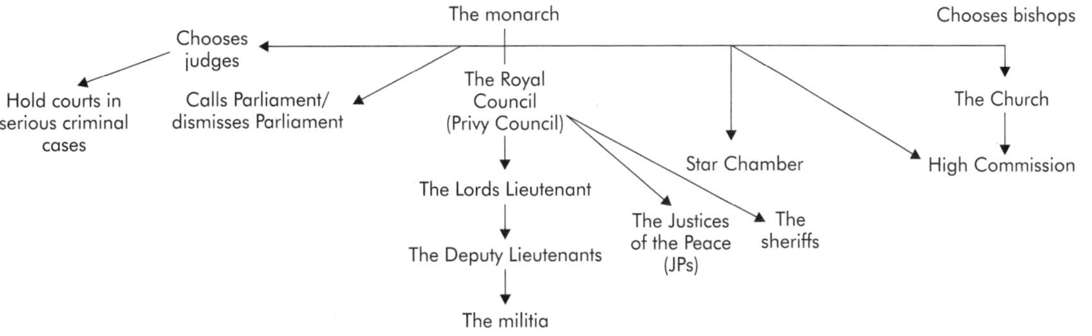

Note: Both Star Chamber and High Commission were Prerogative Courts where the monarch could sit, but usually members of the Royal Council judged.

The structure of government.

- to call and dismiss parliaments,
- to collect certain taxes,
- to issue royal proclamations (instructions) on certain matters.

The monarch was head of the Church, so he appointed bishops and decided on the way the Church of England held its ceremonies and on its doctrines (beliefs). The monarch also had the right to declare war or peace, and was commander of the armed forces. In addition, the day-to-day running of the country was in the monarch's hands: the Royal Council would issue instructions to the JPs and Deputy Lieutenants in the counties under the royal seal, which gave legal authority to them.

Limits to royal power. There were limits to royal power, however, and these limits were a matter for debate throughout the first forty years of the seventeenth century.

- In theory, the monarch should **live of his own.**
- **Royal proclamations** could not override 'common law' – the laws of England that had grown up over hundreds of years.
- The 'subject' (the citizen) of England had rights in law that the monarch could not overrule.

Many of the clashes between kings and parliaments in this period were about the rights of the subject as against the rights of the monarch.

KEY THEMES

'Live of his own' meant that the monarch should not collect taxes in peacetime to support the royal household.

Royal proclamations were new laws declared by the monarch without reference to Parliament.

Royal revenue. Where did the monarch's money come from? The monarch collected customs duties, profits of justice (fines imposed by courts), the rent from Crown lands and some revenue from the Church by right. This was termed 'ordinary revenue'. There were other sources of revenue collected by the Crown such as 'wardship' and 'purveyance' (see pp. 28–9) which caused controversy.

Parliament

Parliament consisted of two houses – the House of Commons and the House of Lords.

House of Lords. The House of Lords consisted of the leading noblemen (peers) (who were members of the aristocracy), the law lords, leading lawyers and some bishops. In the early seventeenth century, the House of Lords (the Upper House) was more important than the House of Commons (the Lower House) and could block any bills (laws) coming to it from the Commons. It tended to support the Crown in disputes with the Commons. The reason why so much of seventeenth-century history seems centred around the House of Commons is that the records of the House of Lords were destroyed in a fire in the 1830s, so historians know far more about the House of Commons.

House of Commons. Unlike the House of Lords, where peers sat by right, the House of Commons was elected. Elections were called by the monarch and supervised locally by the sheriffs. There were two kinds of Member of Parliament:

- County MPs (knights of the shire) who were elected by the 'forty shilling freeholders'. In other words, all those who owned land worth forty shillings (two pounds) were entitled to vote in county elections.
- The burgesses were MPs who represented boroughs – towns that had a charter from the monarch that allowed them to have an MP. The charter laid down who, in each town, was entitled to vote.

Who actually voted? Some boroughs, such as Westminster, had a charter that allowed every male over twenty-one to vote, some other boroughs had a charter that allowed those who owned property to vote, and others were 'closed' boroughs where only the mayor and some leading citizens could vote. Probably 10 to 20 per cent of the population voted normally. In county elections the sheriffs did not, or could not, check who really was a forty shilling freeholder, and probably a lot more people voted than were legally entitled to.

Loyalty of MPs. Most MPs were gentry, but some were lawyers and merchants, especially those holding borough seats.

There were no 'parties' in the modern sense in Parliament. MPs saw themselves as representing their 'countries' (i.e. counties), not any particular party system. They were independent and could be influenced by speeches in Parliament or by royal attitudes and they were proud of the fact that they were independent. Sometimes MPs who shared the same views would get together to try to push their ideas through the House of Commons but there was no 'party system'. There were MPs who, because they had favours from the king, or were councillors, would normally support royal policies in the Commons. However, neither James nor Charles (unlike Elizabeth I) made sure that there were men of enough influence who had respect from other MPs and could be relied on to do this, putting most councillors in the House of Lords.

KEY THEME

Subsidies were a form of taxation based on a valuation of the subject's 'movable goods' – usually amounting to one-tenth or one-fifteenth of the value. Local 'commissioners' (usually JPs) assessed those who could afford to pay, estimating how much their goods were worth.

Only Parliament could vote subsidies, which were the form in which Parliament voted money to the Crown. In theory, Parliament voted subsidies only in cases of emergency, as the king should normally live of his own.

Problems with the valuations on which subsidies were based:

- Rising prices (an important future problem) were not taken into account, so the real worth of subsidies went down.
- The local gentry tended to 'under-assess' their neighbours and friends.

Crown and Parliament – different views on rights and roles

The king's needs for subsidies. Both James and Charles disliked calling Parliament. There had to be a new parliament at the beginning of a new reign but after that parliaments were called only because the Crown wanted **subsidies** for help with financial difficulties.

Parliament's view of its rights. Parliament did not always see its role as being only to vote subsidies, and this was the basis for many of the disputes in the early Stuart parliaments. Parliament claimed certain 'privileges' as rights such as:

- the right to 'free speech',
- freedom from arrest while sitting as an MP,
- the right to settle disputed elections, when there was an argument about a borough charter or who had actually won an election.

Henry VIII and Elizabeth I had, on occasions, let Parliament discuss religion (in theory part of the royal prerogative) and other matters. Parliament also saw itself as having the right to punish corrupt and inefficient royal councillors because this had happened in the Middle Ages.

The Crown's view. The Crown, of course, took a different view of Parliament's rights. Monarchs saw Parliament as being the means to raise subsidies and on occasions bring 'grievances' to the Crown. Parliament had a large number of lawyers, and gentry with legal training, and it often looked back hundreds of years into the past to prove that it had the right to discuss matters that the Crown disliked being discussed, because Parliament had done so in the distant past.

Parliament did not meet regularly and, even in years when Parliament was sitting, the sessions lasted only a few weeks so Parliament was not like a modern parliament, sitting for most of the year doing regular business. Most of society took very little interest in the issues of Parliament. However, there was an established **political nation**.

KEY THEME

The political nation was made up of those who had an interest in politics and what happened in Parliament. This interest was not constant – it appeared at times of elections when there were particular issues that stirred interest.

In a largely illiterate population most people took no part in politics because they did not know about or understand it. However, those in the higher classes, from yeomen upwards, voted and were literate; they comprised what historians call 'the political nation'.

RELIGION IN THE EARLY SEVENTEENTH CENTURY

The importance of religion. Nowadays religious belief is seen as a matter for individuals. This was not so in the seventeenth century. It was impossible to separate religion, politics and royal authority. Religion was central to nearly everyone's view of the world, and religious belief formed the cement that held people's lives together. Christianity had split in the sixteenth century into, at first, Catholic and Protestant. This split had caused a series of terrible religious wars in Europe with each side claiming to be absolutely right.

Two contrasting pictures, one showing the way a Roman Catholic priest dressed (left), the other the way a Puritan minister dressed (right).

Catholics. Roman Catholicism had been the official religion in England until the reign of Henry VIII. In 1563, during the reign of Elizabeth I, England officially became a Protestant country. Although the new Church of England kept some of the ceremonies of the Catholic Church, the Catholic Church did have distinct beliefs.

- Catholics believed that the pope was God's representative on earth, the direct spiritual descendant of Saint Peter, Christ's leading apostle.
- The priest had a very special place. He was thought to have direct communication with God and all Catholics believed they had, on some occasions, to communicate with God through the priest. Therefore he had powers that were not possessed by anyone who was not a priest.
- The priest's special powers were expressed, for example, in the communion service, where it was believed that the bread and wine taken by those receiving communion was literally converted into the body and blood of Jesus Christ.

The pope claimed to be the only authority on what was true in the Christian religion and what was untrue (heresy). This made all Christians spiritual subjects of the pope.

Protestants. Protestantism started in 1517 as a 'protest' against some of the pope's powers. The protest was led by a German monk, Martin Luther. The movement against the Catholic Church spread across Europe. A new set of Christian beliefs emerged which attacked the ideas of the Catholic Church.

- Protestants believed that the pope had no powers over Christians at all; indeed many Protestants saw him as an evil force – the 'anti-Christ'.
- Protestants believed that many of the ceremonies of the Catholic Church were at best unnecessary and at worst evil: the vestments (the elaborate clothing of the priest), the prayers said for the dead, the claim that the bread and wine became the body and blood of Jesus Christ. Protestants believed these were either wrong or at least got in the way of the individual's relationship with God.
- Protestants believed that an individual's relationship with God was based on prayer and reading the Bible. The Catholic Church, on the other hand, disliked the idea of the Bible being read by the laity (the congregation), believing it should be interpreted by the trained mind of the priest. Protestants saw Bible reading as central to discovering religious faith. Therefore all Protestants had their own Bible, most reading from it at least once a day. The 'Word' of the Bible was central to Protestant thinking.
- Protestants also expressed 'the Word' in another way – through the sermon. It was the duty of the minister (the priest, as Catholics called him) to preach the word, rather than to perform glorious ceremonies at an altar cut off from the people. Most important of all, the individual could communicate directly with God through prayer. The 'priest' did not have the monopoly of communication with God.

England had become Protestant during the sixteenth century. Protestantism, because it stressed the individual's

KEY PERSON

John Calvin, who died in 1564, was very important in the development of Protestantism. He established the first extreme Protestant-influenced government in Geneva. His main idea was that of predestination, the belief that individuals are born 'saved' in the eyes of God.

search for God, had tended to break up into different groupings with differing ideas. One of the most important groups were Calvinists named after **John Calvin**. They tended to dislike bishops and wished either to get rid of them altogether or at least to stop them having much authority. Some Protestants wanted no ceremonies at all, just congregations praying together with a preacher, and wanted to get rid of all Church organisation. Others, less extreme, wanted to keep some ceremonies and a proper Church organisation.

The Church of England. The Church of England, set up in 1559 by Elizabeth I, was a compromise between the more extreme Protestant views and the more conservative ones. The queen, like her father Henry VIII, was head of the Church – thus defying the pope's authority. However, some of the old ceremonies were kept and the Church was organised under bishops headed by the Archbishop of Canterbury. This compromise between different views on religion was quite successful because, in practice, Elizabeth appointed bishops of differing views and tried to create a tolerant broad Church that all Protestants could support.

Challenges to the Church of England. By the time James came to the throne, the Church of England was well established but there were two challenges to the 'Elizabethan settlement' of the Church.

- **Roman Catholics.** One came from Roman Catholics who either had never 'converted' to Protestantism, or had been 're-converted' to Catholicism. Catholics, however, made up perhaps 7 per cent of the population and so were never a serious force.
- **Puritans.** More extreme Protestants were a greater challenge to the Church of England (Anglican) settlement. These Protestants thought there were still too many traces of the old Catholic faith in the Anglican Church, and they wanted changes. Some wanted only minor changes, such as to the way the minister dressed for services. The term 'Puritan' covers a range of attitudes, though all Puritans wanted to see an end to anything that could be seen as being Catholic, such as any ceremonies, bishops or authority at all. The term

'Puritan' was also used by some as an insult: for instance, one Archbishop of Canterbury, William Laud, used it to describe anyone who opposed his **high church** view of how the Church of England should be run – a view that many moderates saw as a return to Catholicism. On the other hand, one of James' appointments, Archbishop Abbott, has himself been seen as a Puritan. Rather than seeing all Puritans as extremists wishing to change the Church completely, it is probably safer to see them as more determined Protestants, many of whom were happy to stay in the Church of England under James.

KEY TERMS

High church is the term used to describe the part of the Church of England that continued using Catholic ceremonies and traditions.

Low church describes the part of the Church of England that rejected Catholic traditions and used only Protestant services.

Who were the Puritans? Puritanism was an attitude of mind. It covered a range of different views about Protestantism and the way people should lead their lives. Puritanism was to be found in all social classes; some leading courtiers of Elizabeth's reign were strong Puritans – for instance, the head of Elizabeth's secret service, Walsingham, and her favourite, the Earl of Leicester. Puritanism was less fashionable at court under James because James' court, with its extravagance and sexual scandal, was not, perhaps, as moral as Elizabeth's. Puritans tended to have high moral standards: for instance, they believed that sexual relationships were acceptable only in marriage.

Puritanism seems to have been strongest among the middle classes: among yeoman farmers, some gentry, tradesmen and merchants. Puritanism stressed hard work, being careful with money and being responsible for one's own life in the eyes of God. Puritans saw laziness as a sin against God. Some historians, such as Christopher Hill, have argued that Puritanism was a very attractive attitude of mind to those who were hard working and making their own way in the world. Therefore a yeoman farmer, for example, who was careful with his money and hard working believed that God approved of this, so being a Puritan fitted in with his own way of life. However, Puritanism covered such a wide range of views that the idea that all Puritans objected to any kind of entertainment or celebration would be wrong. Even a strong Puritan such as Oliver Cromwell enjoyed music and dancing.

Where was Puritanism strongest? Puritanism was strongest in London and East Anglia. It seems to have been less popular in the north, where Roman Catholicism was still quite strong, especially in Lancashire. In the cloth-making towns of the west of England, such as Taunton and Gloucester, Puritanism was also strong among the trading classes, such as weavers and merchants. In the countryside in Devon, Cornwall and Somerset, Puritanism was not so strong. The country people seem to have held on to their traditional festivals, such as May Day, which were disapproved of by Puritans, who thought all these celebrations were sinful in the eyes of God and took people away from work.

Anti-Catholicism. This was one of the strongest forces in English life in the seventeenth century. For most English people, Catholicism was associated with the burnings of Protestants under Mary, with massacres of Protestants abroad (of course, Protestants had also massacred Catholics) and, above all, with England's traditional enemies Spain and France. The object of the Spanish Armada of 1588 had been the re-conversion, by force, of England to Catholicism, and the 'absolute' monarchs of Europe, who saw Catholicism as part of their authoritarian system, seemed at odds with 'English liberty'. English Catholics were seen as dangerous because their first loyalty, in theory, was to the pope, 'a foreign prince', not to the English king. Catholicism was therefore seen as unpatriotic, religiously evil, and the driving force behind England's enemies. Anti-Catholic attitudes were deeply rooted in English society from the top to the bottom and could unite people in a way that nothing else could. The Gunpowder Plot of 1605 (see pp. 47–9) of course served only to confirm this prejudice in the public mind.

Court and country. To some extent, religious division was associated with a division between court and country. During the seventeenth century there was a split in attitudes between those gentry who lived on their country estates, rarely coming up to London, and the court surrounding the king. Sir Walter Raleigh summed up the anger felt towards the court when he said, 'Say to the court it shines and glows like rotten wood.' The puritan-minded country gentry saw the court as devoted to luxury, hideously expensive and corrupt. They suspected that the court was inclined to Roman Catholicism, and that courtiers were at court only to get 'offices of profit' and pensions. The 'country' saw themselves as honest, patriotic and having the interests of their counties and the countryside, in which they lived, at heart. Their resentment of rich London 'money men' and courtiers was part of the tension that surfaced in seventeenth-century politics and parliaments.

SUMMARY QUESTIONS

1 What were the prerogatives of the monarch?

2 What were the rights and role of Parliament?

3 What were the differences in beliefs between Catholics and Protestants?

4 Why were so many English people anti-Catholic?

5 What did 'Puritans' believe?

CHAPTER 2

James I's reign 1603–25

INTRODUCTION

James I had been King of Scotland as James VI. He was the son of Mary Queen of Scots and the great-great-grandson of Henry VII of England. He was offered the throne on the death of Elizabeth I, who died in 1603 without an heir. Although a Scot, he was a Protestant which was, for Parliament, a most important aspect of his character. However, there were other aspects of his character which were to have an important influence on how he ran the state.

- **The wisest fool in Christendom?** James has been criticised by historians in the past. His knowledge and intelligence have been made little of; he has been seen as an educated man of no real practical sense.
  A contemporary remark about him, 'The wisest fool in Christendom', is often quoted. To be fair to James, he had a difficult childhood. His mother, Mary Queen of Scots, was executed by Elizabeth I in 1587 and he found himself bullied by a series of tutors and advisers until he came of age. As James VI of Scotland he was successful, managing to balance all the religious and political rivalries in a divided kingdom. He was highly intelligent and well educated, although he was perhaps too fond of showing it, and his experience in ruling Scotland led him to believe that 'as a wise and experienced king' he would have no difficulties in England.
- **Fear of assassination.** He disliked war but was a keen huntsman, taking considerable risks while riding. Thus those who saw his pacifism as cowardice may well have been mistaken. On the other hand, the Gunpowder Plot certainly panicked him, and he lived in fear of assassination, wearing a rapier-proof doublet – a padded jacket. (A rapier was a small sword.)

James I, King of England, 1603–25.

- **Personal preferences.** His main weaknesses were handsome young men and spending too much money. His interest in young men was not lost on his contemporaries and the inevitable rumours of homosexuality did not help to raise his esteem. The main problem with both Robert Carr (later the Earl of Somerset) and even more with George Villiers (later the Duke of Buckingham), the two main **favourites** of James, was that he allowed them real political power and influence.
- **Extravagance.** Scotland was a relatively poor country and from the beginning of his reign James saw England as a land of 'milk and honey'. From the start of his reign

KEY TERM

Favourites were those courtiers who had a particularly close and influential relationship with the king. They were not just private companions. In Buckingham's case, as will be seen, he was chief minister and virtually controlled the court.

he spent a lot of money, not only on himself but on gifts and pensions to courtiers. Many of these courtiers were Scotsmen who had accompanied him to England and their lavish lifestyle became a source of resentment and scandal. Of course, English courtiers also shared in James' generosity. His extravagance was probably the main weakness in his character, and he never understood that, however rich England was compared to Scotland, his income was still limited.

- **Political skills.** James can, however, be seen as quite clever. Although he believed in the divine right of kings, he seems to have realised that he should not try to be an **absolute monarch** in his relations with Parliament. Despite clashes, he usually did not push too far and, as an able politician, knew the art of the possible. His wife, Anne of Denmark, lived apart from the court for much of the time and does not seem to have had much influence. Much was expected of his first son, Prince Henry, but he died in 1612. Charles, his second son, seems to have led a fairly withdrawn life until the 1620s; he shared his father's belief in divine right but lacked both his father's shrewdness and his elder brother's ability to arouse admiration among the 'political nation'.
- **James' intelligence.** On two issues he was ahead of his time. He hated smoking and wrote a long attack on the health risks that went with it, even mentioning the black tar that was found in the lungs of smokers. He came to disbelieve in witches at a time when the majority of the population still believed in witchcraft and its powers.

KEY TERM

Absolute monarch. An absolute monarch was a ruler who ruled without Parliament. Many European countries at this time, including France, had absolute monarchies.

The situation on James' accession to the throne in 1603

- **Spanish War.** On Elizabeth's death England was at war with Spain. However, the war had become a stalemate. A campaign against Catholic Spanish-backed rebels in Ireland was coming to a successful conclusion.
- **Finances.** Elizabeth had been financially careful, so the royal household had been running within budget. There were debts caused by the wars, but parliamentary subsidies were still coming in to cover these. Therefore, the financial situation was, in the short term, healthy. In the long term, however, potential problems loomed. Subsidies were not increasing enough in value; neither were the rents from Crown lands keeping pace with

rising prices. So inflation was making the Crown poorer. James' extravagance (see below) made the situation much worse.

- **Government ministers.** James inherited his chief minister, **Robert Cecil**, from Elizabeth. Cecil was a very competent minister and administrator and James was fortunate to have him in control when he came to the throne. He was also a ruthless politician who seized every opportunity to eliminate rivals at court. He was the son of Elizabeth's famous chief minister, Burghley, and a very cunning clever politician, though perhaps not a great reformer.
- **Religion.** In religion, some of the 'puritan' element hoped for Church reform from James, who had come from a strongly Protestant country, while at the same time Catholics hoped that James would relax the **penal laws** against Catholics, allowing them to worship in

KEY PERSON

Robert Cecil. It was Cecil who organised the smooth transition of power from Elizabeth to James. As a result he was the most important person in English government (apart from the king) from 1603 to 1612. His successes included

- negotiating peace with Spain in 1604,
- resolving the Gunpowder Plot,
- extending the Book of Rates in 1608.

His skill was in keeping James' spending down to an acceptable level. In many ways he was, as one historian has written, 'a servant far nobler and more able than James deserved'.

Robert Cecil, Earl of Salisbury and Chief Minister 1603–12.

KEY TERM

Penal laws. Everyone had to attend Anglican Church on Sundays. The penal laws, aimed at Catholics, made it illegal not to; each time they failed to attend, Catholics could be fined. Those Catholics who did not go to Church were called recusants. Some rich Catholic gentry were made an example of by the Royal Council and were fined heavily. Sir Thomas Tresham, in Northamptonshire, had paid £8,000 in the 1580s and 1590s.

KEY PERSON

Sir Walter Raleigh. An Elizabethan adventurer and courtier, Raleigh was to remain in prison until 1616. While in prison he wrote a *History of the World.*

private, and not forcing them to attend Anglican services.

- **Privileges.** Parliament was anxious to establish that James understood its 'privileges' (as MPs saw them) since the Scottish Parliament, in the kingdom that he came from, had very few powers.
- **Opposition in court.** There were those who opposed James being offered the throne. The Main Plot was a plot to remove James from the throne and replace him with a cousin, Arabella Stuart. This plot was put together by some of the leading noblemen, including Lord Cobham and Lord Grey. It failed, and many of those involved in the plot, such as **Sir Walter Raleigh**, were imprisoned.

JAMES' FIRST PARLIAMENT 1604–10

Goodwin v Fortesque. James' first parliament started with a dispute over which member had been elected for Buckinghamshire. One candidate was Sir John Fortesque, a royal councillor whom the council and the king wanted to have in the House of Commons. The other candidate was Sir Francis Goodwin, who had actually won the election. However, the Court of Chancery, which James claimed had the right to decide in disputed elections (because Chancery sent out the writs to the sheriffs calling them), had decided that Goodwin was not able to take his seat as an MP because he had been outlawed for not paying his debts. Parliament claimed that it alone had the right to decide in disputed elections. At first James stood for the right of the Court of Chancery to decide the case, because he saw a challenge to his royal prerogative. In the end, both 'sides' compromised on James' suggestion. The compromise was that both Goodwin and Fortesque were declared not elected and a new election was held. Also, most importantly from Parliament's point of view, James accepted that Parliament should be the judge in disputed elections.

Shirley's case. At the same time, another important case regarding parliamentary privilege was settled. Shirley, an MP, had been arrested for debt, and Parliament sent the

Governor of the Fleet debtors' prison to the Tower until Shirley was released. This case established, finally, what Parliament had claimed for some time – that Members of Parliament, while Parliament was actually sitting, had freedom from arrest, except in cases of treason, serious crime (felony) or breach of the peace.

The proposed union of England and Scotland. In 1603 Scotland and England were separate countries and this was the first time a King of England had been King of Scotland as well. Legally this did not make them one country. James, as King of Scotland as well as England, had set his heart on a union.

The House of Commons was not enthusiastic about union with Scotland. There was much prejudice against the Scots as a backward nation, and a union of the two kingdoms would be complicated because Scottish law was very different from English law. The House of Lords proposed, after a conference with the Commons, that commissioners (representatives) should be appointed to discuss the various issues that union would involve with similar commissioners for Scotland. The House of Commons was divided and, as the days went by, opposition to union mounted. A leading member of the House, Sir Edwin Sandys, attacked the proposed new title of Great Britain: 'By this name the Kingdom of England is dissolved.' The judges who were consulted argued that the new title would mean 'an utter extinction of all the laws now in force'.

The matter dragged on until 1607, involving such issues as the problems of Scottish and English law and the status of those born in Scotland after or before James' accession to the English throne. In the end the proposed union was blocked on these legal issues, and James was bitterly disappointed.

Purveyance. When purveyance was the subject of a petition from Parliament to James, he made a tactful reply promising to look into cases of corruption. The Lords made a radical proposal that the whole system should end, and in exchange the Crown should be voted £50,000 per annum in compensation. The Commons were divided on

KEY THEME

James' attitude to union of England and Scotland. James tried very hard to convince the English Parliament of the benefits of union between the two kingdoms. He said in his address to the new Parliament in 1604:

'Hath not God first united these two Kingdoms both in language, religion and similitude of manners . . . Hath he not made us all in one Island?'

KEY TERM

Purveyance was the right of the Crown to buy goods for the royal household at a discount well below the market price. Also there was the right to take carts and horses to transport the goods. The system was open to abuse and corruption and had been widely attacked in Elizabeth's reign. It was, however, part of the royal prerogative and monarchs had been extremely reluctant to give up what they saw as their valuable rights.

how to solve the problem, but the general view was that £50,000 was far too much and £20,000 was suggested. Robert Cecil realised that this would be quite inadequate compensation for the valuable right of buying all goods for the royal household at a bargain price. On the other hand, some MPs thought the system so corrupt than no compensation should be paid. In the end, although James issued a proclamation 'for prevention of abuses in purveyance' and had some royal agents punished, there was no agreement on purveyance. Cecil hoped to introduce the scheme to deal with purveyance in the 1604 and 1606–7 parliaments. However, at both times the scheme failed to be accepted because of complaints about the king's extravagance and debate about union with Scotland.

Wardship. This was another grievance of Parliament that was a result of a very old right of the Crown. If a landowner died before his children reached twenty-one they became wards of the Crown. In simple terms, in theory, the Crown looked after them and ran the estate. In practice, the right to be the guardian of a 'ward of court' was sold and whoever became the guardian could make a profit out of the ward's estate until he, or she, became twenty-one. Usually, of course, relatives would buy the right to wardship from the Court of Wards to prevent the estate falling into the hands of someone who did not have the family's interest at heart. Fathers had to leave money in their wills to allow for the purchase of the wardship of their own children. The whole system dated from feudal times when, in theory, all landowners held their land as tenants of the king, but by the seventeenth century it had become an outdated and hated system which put money into the pockets of the officers of the Court of Wards, and into the royal purse. Wardship was worth about £60,000 a year to the Crown. In addition, the officers of the Court of Wards received 'presents' or outright bribes to help people secure wardships.

The Commons proposed to 'buy out' the royal right to wardships and abolish the Court of Wards. The king did not take kindly to this suggestion, which he saw as attacking his prerogative, and he sent a sharp reply to the House of Commons.

Impositions: Bates' case 1606. Impositions were extra customs duties, and the collection of customs contributed to the king's revenue. The question was whether the Crown could impose extra duties on goods in addition to the accepted customs duties. John Bates, a London merchant with the Levant Company, refused to pay duty on an import of currants. The matter went to the Court of the Exchequer and Bates lost. The result was that a whole new set of impositions could be set on imports, thus giving the treasury a real 'windfall'. Parliament objected, seeing impositions as a 'back-door' tax that they had no control over.

By 1606 the Commons had decided to present a summing up of what they saw as their rights, which dated back for hundreds of years – the **Apology of the House of Commons.**

The Apology of the House of Commons. After some of these preliminary clashes with James, MPs were anxious to ensure that the king understood the rights of the Commons.

- They asserted that their privileges were under threat, quoting problems over free speech and disputed elections.
- They declared that free speech, free election and freedom from arrest were their 'right and due inheritance'.
- They asserted that the king could not make changes in religion without the consent of Parliament.
- Purveyance and wardship were mentioned.

James' expenditure. The cost of the royal household rose from £64,000 a year in 1603 to £114,000 a year by 1610. In the same period, the amount spent on the royal wardrobe went up from £9,000 to £36,000. James had a wife and children, but it was still a startling leap. However, the real spending was on favourites and courtiers. James Hay, Earl of Carlisle, was perhaps the most extravagant of the early favourites. He invented the 'double supper' – the ultimate in **conspicuous consumption**. A splendid supper of twenty courses was laid in front of his guests then simply thrown away before they could eat it, to be replaced

KEY THEME

The Apology of the House of Commons. The document can be seen as Parliament asserting itself, but it also made the point that 'the prerogatives of Princes may easily, and daily grow . . . the privileges of the subject are for the most part at an everlasting stand'. In other words, kings were becoming more powerful and the Commons saw themselves as protecting the rights of the subject; the tone was defensive rather than aggressive. It appears that the apology was never formally presented to the king, but he probably saw a copy.

by an even more extravagant meal. Hay calculated that he received £400,000 from the Crown, but he died penniless.

On average, during the first ten years of the reign, James was giving away between £60,000 and £80,000 a year on gifts and pensions to courtiers. In 1606 the Lord Treasurer, Lord Cecil, sold off areas of land owned by the Crown because by 1606 Crown debt stood at £750,000. Crown lands worth nearly three-quarters of a million pounds were sold, and subsidies came in, even in a time of peace, but the debt was still £280,000 in 1610. James was so pleased to get a parliamentary subsidy in 1606 that, to celebrate, he immediately gave three Scottish courtiers £44,000 and spent £800 on decorations for the uniforms of the Royal Guards.

Not only did this conspicuous consumption give the court a bad name among the more modest gentry, but it also put some of the aristocracy into debt. When they had financial difficulties, their local and national influence and power declined. In political terms, the possible decline of aristocratic wealth and influence may have had some effect in increasing the self-confidence of the gentry.

Finance and the 'Great Contract' of 1610

James was incapable of living within his means. In theory, he could not ask Parliament for a subsidy in peacetime and therefore he had to look at all possible ways of increasing his income. These included:

- customs duties,
- 'feudal dues' (wardship, purveyance),
- rent from Crown lands.

The first Treasurer, **Thomas Sackville** (Earl of Dorset), was fairly incompetent. It was Robert Cecil, made Earl of Salisbury in 1605 (Treasurer after Dorset's death), who made the efforts, such as they were, to keep James' finances afloat. He was constantly hampered by James' determination to give out more gifts and pensions.

Customs farmers. Cecil was responsible for increasing the revenue of the Court of Wards and the sale of Crown

KEY TERM

Conspicuous consumption. James overspent considerably on entertainment, and it was important for people at his court to show how rich they were. Expensive entertaining was an obvious way of doing this. One banquet of Hay's, in 1621, cost £3,300 and involved one hundred cooks preparing 1,600 separate dishes including pheasants, partridges, larks, swans, two whole pigs and six 2-metre-long salmon. Some aristocrats and courtiers went even further; later in the century the first Lord Coleraine choked to death trying to swallow the entire rump of a turkey. Clothes were also part of the show that a courtier or aristocrat had to pay for, to keep up appearances. The Duke of Buckingham was spending £3,000 per year on clothes by 1627.

KEY PERSON

Thomas Sackville. Such was his corruption that he was nick-named 'Fill-Sack' in reference to how he used to fill his pockets.

Thomas Sackville, Earl of Dorset, Treasurer, 1561–1608.

lands for the sum of £645,952. The collection of customs was 'privatised'; London money-lenders and merchants formed groups to bid for the right to collect the customs duties. These 'customs farmers' then paid the Crown a fixed sum and their profit was what they could collect above that sum.

With the new impositions (extra customs duties) Salisbury was able to increase the rent paid by the customs farmers, because the value of the customs duties was higher. The customs farmers, such as William Garway and Nicholas Salter, also lent money to the Crown in advance of when the rent was due. The customs farmers were much disliked by the other merchants and the system itself was resented. However, by 1611 Salisbury was getting £200,000 per annum more from customs than in 1605.

The Great Contract. Salisbury was a cautious man, perhaps rather unimaginative, but he did come up with one scheme which might have transformed the royal finances: the Great Contract of 1610. Basically, Salisbury's idea, not in itself a new one, was this:

- The Crown would give up the right to feudal dues, such as wardship and purveyance (which were always a source of friction with parliaments), in exchange for a fixed sum per annum to be raised in taxation.
- In addition he needed a lump sum to pay off royal debts.

Very reluctantly, Parliament offered £200,000, after a lot of argument, to cover the loss of feudal dues. MPs were suspicious of the idea of giving James an additional annual income as it might make him 'independent' of Parliament: if he had enough money he would not need to call Parliament again. So, however much Parliament complained about James' extravagance, in a way it was in their interests that James remained short of money. Also they thought that James should economise and resented having to vote more money that would come from their constituents, who were making it clear that they objected.

James' doubts. On the other hand, James too had his doubts about the contract. His Chancellor of the Exchequer, the wonderfully named Sir Julius Caesar, thought Salisbury had got his sums wrong and that £200,000 would not be enough. Also James objected to bargaining with the House of Commons about his prerogative rights, thinking that it was beneath his dignity. The contract was finally sunk when James made a demand for another £200,000 lump sum. The House of Commons refused this outright so James dismissed Parliament, without any solution to the Crown's financial problem in sight.

Salisbury lost most of his influence with James and died in 1612.

THE YEARS WITHOUT PARLIAMENT 1610–21

With the exception of the brief failure of the Addled Parliament, these years saw no parliaments and, in some ways, can be seen as years of drift with no real direction of policy. Much of what happened can be explained in terms of **court faction** (rivalry) between groups of courtiers around the king who wished to gain offices of profit and to influence James.

The 'Addled Parliament' of 1614. It got off to a bad start because MPs thought the Crown had been interfering with elections through 'undertakers' – courtiers who had undertaken (promised) to get MPs who were friendly to the court elected. James needed money, as usual, and asked for a subsidy to cover the costs of the funeral of Henry, his eldest son who had died in 1612, and the costs of the marriage of his daughter Elizabeth. The House of Commons was not sympathetic, presenting instead petitions about impositions. Bishop Neile of Lincoln, a supporter of the court, attacked the Commons from the House of Lords. The Commons replied with an attack on him. The debates became disorganised attacks on the court and still no subsidies were voted. James' attitude is shown in his conversation with the Spanish ambassador, Sarmiento (Count Gondomar): 'The House of Commons is a body without a head. The members gave their opinions in a disorderly manner ... I am surprised my ancestors should ever have permitted such an institution to come into existence. I am a stranger [here] and found it when I arrived, so I am obliged to put up with what I cannot get rid of.'

James could not 'get rid of' Parliament but, as it voted no subsidies, it was dissolved in June 1614 and not called again until 1621.

KEY TERMS

Court faction. The royal court was not a united group of courtiers wishing to serve the king. There were always rivalries between groups of courtiers, either over personal issues and ambitions or over disagreements on matters of policy such as foreign affairs or religion. The most important factions were dominated by the leading families of the time: the Howards and the Pembrokes. These factions often hoped to control or influence the king's most intimate friends or favourites. A favourite, such as Carr or Buckingham, could persuade the king to appoint a courtier to a position with a salary (an office of profit) or to give a courtier a pension.

Court faction centred around money, principles and personal feuds.

Addled Parliament. The name given to this parliament refers to an 'addled' – rotten – egg. The parliament lasted only a few weeks and achieved nothing.

The Overbury scandal 1615–16. Robert Carr, the royal favourite, now Earl of Rochester, was having an affair with Lady Essex. His friend, who had helped the affair along and knew all its details, was Sir Thomas Overbury. Lady Essex managed to get an annulment of her marriage to the Earl of Essex, leaving her free to marry Rochester. Overbury, although he had been happy to arrange the affair, tried to persuade Rochester not to marry her. James tried to get Overbury out of the way by offering him an ambassadorship abroad. Overbury refused, and James was persuaded to send him to the Tower on a very doubtful charge. In 1615 Lady Essex, now Rochester's wife, sent Overbury, in the Tower, a poisoned pie. Eventually both Rochester and his wife were charged with murder, but James pardoned them.

The scandal had two effects. Firstly, it finished Rochester as James' favourite – he was already being edged out by George Villiers, Duke of Buckingham. Secondly, as the story became public knowledge, it lowered respect for both James and his court.

The rise of George Villiers, Duke of Buckingham.
Key points:

- Between 1618 and his assassination in 1628, Villiers (created Duke of Buckingham in 1623) was Chief Minister and the most influential man in England.
- Buckingham created a great deal of resentment among the country gentry because of his complete control of patronage (the granting of favours, pensions, titles) from the Crown. If you fell out with Buckingham there was no future career open to you.
- He also increased the sale of titles of honour until it became a public scandal: knighthoods, baronies, even earldoms, were sold. As the market became 'flooded' the price went down. Knighthoods were sold for £30. Most of the 'old' nobility and gentry objected to their titles being degraded by the sale of titles.
- He was largely responsible for foreign policy throughout this period. He seems to have had no fixed principles, at first being in favour of a peaceful policy towards Spain, later pushing for war.

George Villiers, first Duke of Buckingham and Chief Minister 1618–28.

- He transferred his affections from James to Charles as it became obvious that James had not much longer to live.

Factions fight for control. The rise of Buckingham was the result of the divisions at court, and of the fall from favour of Rochester. As Robert Carr, the Earl of Rochester, lost influence with James, rival factions at court tried to interest James in a new favourite, a young man who would be under their influence.

- The **Howard** faction, led by the Earl of Northampton, were pro-Catholic and pro-Spanish.
- The **anti-Howard** faction, which included Abbott, the Archbishop of Canterbury, wanted to stop James'

increasingly pro-Spanish policy. They put forward the young son of a country gentleman, **George Villiers**, who, at this stage, gave the impression that he would do the bidding of the anti-Howard faction. By 1618, however, he did not need any backers at court; his influence with James was so strong that all the court had to defer to him.

Finance remained a problem. During the years of the Howard influence at court (1611–16) corruption was rife. Suffolk, the Lord Treasurer, was not only incompetent, but dishonest. He was also unable to stop James spending above his income. By 1616 the deficit on ordinary revenue had reached £160,000. In other words, James was building up a huge debt.

The Cockayne Project and the City of London 1615–17. One of the ways to raise greater revenue was to increase trade. In 1615 Alderman Cockayne, a city merchant and a friend of the Howard faction, came up with a plan that was to be a disaster for trade. He argued that instead of exporting half-finished cloth to northern Europe, where it was finished, England should export more finished cloth. The cloth trade to northern Europe was in the hands of the Merchant Adventurers, a company based in the City of London. Cockayne persuaded James that they should have their monopoly taken away and that it should be given to a new company that would be 'go ahead' and 'modern', exporting more finished cloth. This company would, of course, be headed by Cockayne, who 'oiled the wheels' with James by lending him £10,000. The new company was called the King's Merchant Adventurers. The whole scheme was not well planned. Cockayne's associates did not have enough money to buy the wool, and did not have the expertise to make finished cloth, or the contacts abroad to sell it.

By 1618 the cloth trade had collapsed, which led to social distress among sheep farmers and weavers. James had to restore the Merchant Adventurers' monopoly, but they, in turn, had to pay £10,000 to get what they saw as their rights back. War broke out in Europe in 1618 as the Merchant Adventurers were trying to re-establish their

KEY PERSON

George Villiers, Duke of Buckingham. Villiers was a favourite of James who rose quickly to prominence after 1615. As Carr's influence declined in 1616, because of the Overbury murder, and after the Howards were removed from power in 1618 so Buckingham (he was made Duke of Buckingham in 1617) became more important.

His misuse of the system of honours turned gentry sympathies away from the Crown. Buckingham's weakness was that he misunderstood the nature of the opposition to him in the House of Commons. He was to survive James' death in 1625 but was assassinated in 1628.

KEY THEME

Corruption. Profits of office. Suffolk built a great house, Audley End in Essex, which James described as 'too large for a king, it might do for a Lord Treasurer'.

trade, and the export of cloth to northern Europe never again reached its 1614 level. War was one of the reasons for this, but the City of London, which had been prepared to lend to James in the past, never really trusted him again, blaming the collapse of the cloth trade on James' association with Cockayne; gradually, loans to the Crown from the City dried up. This process continued in the 1620s as Buckingham interfered with the privileges of the chartered companies. By 1625 the great companies, such as the Levant Company and the East India Company, had

Engraving of a patent monopolist from 1624.

ceased to look to the Crown to protect them and had ceased to be lenders to the Crown.

Financial reform 1618–20. Suffolk fell from power in 1618 as the Howards lost their grip at court to the rising favourite, Buckingham. The Treasury was put into commission (run by a committee) that was packed with anti-Howard-faction members. They managed to make savings in the cost of running the navy, the royal household and the wardrobe. However, despite this, royal debt rose in one year by £100,000 to £800,000. Sir Francis Bacon, the Lord Chancellor, tried to cut back pensions by giving **patents of monopoly** instead, but the new broom that was to dominate royal finances was Lionel Cranfield, a London merchant whom Buckingham had brought in to reform finances. At first, in charge of the wardrobe, he insisted on economies and on paying cash to get discounts, thus saving £20,000 per annum.

KEY TERM

Monopolies. In theory, monopolies were granted to those who had invented a new product or process; they gave inventors the exclusive right to manufacture or sell their invention for a period of years, thus repaying them for their efforts. However, even under Elizabeth 'patents' of monopoly had been abused, courtiers being given the exclusive right to sell products, or to license others to sell them. Courtiers were not interested in selling playing cards, soap or glass; they made their profits by selling licences to the companies that produced or sold the products. Without a licence, a product that was subject to a patent of monopoly could not be sold. Monopolies became a way of rewarding courtiers and were much resented by the merchants and the general public, who had to pay higher prices.

THE FINAL YEARS 1621–5

The parliament of 1621. The parliament of 1621 met in difficult times.

- It was a time of economic depression, caused by the Thirty Years' War and the consequent fall in exports to a devastated Europe.
- There was a very bad harvest in 1621 which caused widespread distress.
- There was wide support for an anti-Spanish foreign policy.

The MPs were very well aware of the situation facing their constituents. As one MP said, 'All grievances are trifles compared with the decay of trade.' The country gentry attacked the great London chartered companies, who were blamed for having a monopoly of trade and strangling other ports outside London.

The main attack, however, was on those who held monopolies (monopolists), such as Sir Giles Mompesson and Sir Francis Mitchell, who were impeached (tried and convicted by the Commons) for their corrupt practices in monopolies such as **licensing alehouses**.

The fall of Lord Chancellor Bacon. The Commons then turned on Sir Francis Bacon, encouraged by Sir Edward Coke, the great common lawyer who had been dismissed as Lord Chief Justice by James in 1616 for supporting the independence of judges and the importance of common law (law made by Parliament) against prerogative law (law made by the king). Bacon was an old court rival of Coke, so old scores were being paid off. The Commons saw Bacon as a symbol of court corruption and mismanagement because of his gifts of monopolies, and actually impeached him for taking bribes as Lord Chancellor. Bacon was fined £40,000 and briefly imprisoned.

KEY TERM

Licensing of alehouses. Many alehouses were illegal gambling dens or partly brothels. Local Justices of the Peace were anxious to ensure that they were properly licensed and controlled. Mompesson's patent, to control licensing, should, in theory, have helped with this. In practice, Mompesson's agents used their powers to run a protection racket where the illegal practices were covered up in exchange for a payment. What was worse from Parliament's point of view was that the JPs were forced, because of the royal patent, to co-operate with Mompesson's agents.

Sir Edward Coke, MP for Liskeard, Cornwall, in the parliament of 1621.

The challenge of the Puritans. The challenge of the Puritans was not significant in the period 1618–25 in terms of attacks on the Church of England, although some Puritans with very strong convictions made the decision to go to America. The most famous of these sailed in the *Mayflower* in 1620. These Puritans were a very small minority who were Independents, that is they would not accept any church organisation that included bishops. Most Puritans were content to stay within the Church and the issue for them was the great struggle going on in Europe between the Catholics and Protestants in the Thirty Years' War. Some believed that England was the nation chosen by God to lead the Protestants of Europe against the Catholics. These members of the gentry, such as **Sir Edward Coke** and Sir Robert Phelips in Parliament, therefore, were unhappy with James' foreign policy. The Commons were anxious to support the Elector Palatine, who was married to James' daughter and was seen by many of the country gentry as a Protestant hero. So they called for war with Spain, although they voted only two subsidies for military support to recover the Palatinate, which was quite inadequate because the Spanish army was the most powerful in Europe.

James was annoyed at the Commons discussing foreign policy, which was part of the royal prerogative, and therefore ordered them to stop doing so. On 18 December the Commons produced a **remonstrance** (a statement) to the king, arguing that their ancient right of free speech allowed them to discuss any matter regardless of the royal prerogative. James' reply was to dismiss Parliament in January 1622 saying that they were attacking his fundamental rights.

Lionel Cranfield and royal finances. Cranfield became Lord Treasurer in October 1621. His rise was swift (backed, at this stage, by Buckingham) and he became Earl of Middlesex in 1622.

Middlesex realised that the only way James could be financially sound would be by cutting expenditure, preventing him giving gifts and pensions to courtiers and making economies in his lifestyle. At the same time he

KEY PEOPLE

Sir Edward Coke was a lawyer and judge who refused to be bullied by the king. In 1616 he was dismissed as Lord Chief Justice. In 1621 he was elected to Parliament as MP for Liskeard in Cornwall.

The **remonstrance** of 1621 was proposed by Coke and he was imprisoned for seven months as a result. He returned to Parliament in 1624 as MP for Coventry. In 1628 he drafted the Petition of Right (see pp. 67–8). He died in 1634 as the champion of English common law.

Lionel Cranfield, Earl of Middlesex. Cranfield was James' most successful finance minister. As a merchant financier he was a wealthy man and was appointed in charge of customs in 1613. In two years he managed to increase revenue by £30,000 a year. He also increased income from wardships by 25 per cent from 1619 to 1625. In 1624 he was sacked as Lord Treasurer for opposing war with Spain (see p. 43).

managed, even during a trade depression, to get more money from the customs farmers. However, the business-like Middlesex faced an impossible task.

- He knew that England could not afford war with Spain and therefore was in favour of a peaceful policy.
- James, despite promising Middlesex that he would give out no more gifts and pensions, continued to do so, leaving Middlesex to refuse to actually pay the pensions or gifts. This made him very unpopular with the courtiers.
- Even peace with Spain was expensive. The cost of the 'Spanish match' trip of Charles and Buckingham was over £100,000, with nothing to show for it (see p. 53).

When Charles and Buckingham returned from Madrid, intent on war with Spain, Middlesex knew that England could not afford it unless Parliament voted for more in subsidies than it had ever done before. He tried to persuade James to oppose war but he had now made an enemy of Buckingham: firstly, because he tried to limit James' gifts to Buckingham's allies at court, and secondly, because Buckingham was determined on war with Spain, a popular policy in the country.

The 1624 parliament. Certain facts influenced what happened during this parliament.

- By 1624 James was ill and Charles and Buckingham were virtually in control. James was convinced that their policy of war with Spain, however temporarily popular, would be a disaster, but he no longer had the strength to oppose them.
- He knew that Middlesex was the only Lord Treasurer he had had who could deal with the royal finances competently, but as Middlesex had made lots of enemies with the City merchants (through higher customs), the country gentry (through increased wardship charges) and the court (by refusing to pay pensions), James lacked the strength to defend him.
- James was shrewd enough to realise that Charles and Buckingham's policy of allowing Parliament to discuss foreign policy in 1624, a move that was a result of their

being 'carried away' by their new found popularity, would store up trouble for the future. 'You will live to have your belly full of parliaments', he told Charles. Again, he now lacked the strength to do more than merely protest. By the time Parliament met in February 1624, power was slipping from James' hands.

Parliament's reluctance to fund war. Parliament was prepared to vote money to recover the Palatinate from Spain, but did not favour a direct military attack on the Spanish occupying forces. It wanted to return to the Elizabethan way of waging war against Spain – at sea. If the Spanish treasure fleets from South America could be captured then Spain would be unable to pay her armies, they argued. A small 'diversionary' attack in the Spanish Netherlands was the only land campaign that the country gentry would agree to.

KEY EVENT

The impeachment of Cranfield. Again Sir Edward Coke (who thought that he should have been Lord Treasurer) took the lead, but the real driving force behind the fall of Middlesex was Buckingham, who now feared the competence of Middlesex as well as resenting his economies at court. The Commons were happy to attack the Lord Treasurer because of his new customs duties and his 'pro-Spanish' attitudes as they saw them. James failed to defend Middlesex, the only competent Treasurer that he had had during the last ten years. Middlesex was heavily fined (£50,000) and briefly imprisoned. The attack on Middlesex may well also have been motivated by the fear that a competent Treasurer would make the Crown financially so secure that it would no longer be necessary to call Parliament.

James said that the war must be fought in Europe, and before it could start he not only required the subsidies to fight it, but nearly £1 million to pay off his debts. Charles and Buckingham virtually ignored this and gave promises to the Commons that Parliament would appoint commissioners to oversee the spending of any money raised for the war, and that Parliament could decide how the war was fought. Given these promises, the Commons voted subsidies worth £300,000 – not enough for serious attacks on Spain in Europe. The other main business of the 1624 parliament was **the impeachment of Lionel Cranfield**, Earl of Middlesex.

Monopolies. Monopolies were still seen by Parliament as being one of the most important issues. Members finally dealt with the problem, they thought, by pushing through the Statute of Monopolies, which made monopolies that were not concerned with new inventions illegal. In theory, therefore, only new inventions could be protected by a monopoly given to the inventor to reward him for his efforts. However, in the 1630s monopolies were to reappear by twisting the law.

The death of James 1625. James, still reluctant to start a war with Spain that did not involve a direct attempt to recover the Palatinate by ground troops, refrained from actually taking any action whatsoever, to the frustration of Charles and Buckingham. Parliament began to suspect that they would not fulfil the promises they had made to Parliament regarding the proposed war. While he lived, James still retained some power to influence events, or at least to prevent the war he feared, but on 27 March 1625 he died at his huge mansion of Theobalds. Now Charles and Buckingham could do as they wished.

RELIGION

Puritan demands. At the beginning of the reign, the 'puritan' element in the Church of England had organised themselves to petition James for changes in church services. The result was the Millenary Petition of 1603, so called because it was claimed that it represented the views of a thousand ministers.

- They asked for an end to confirmation, to the sign of the cross in baptism, to the ring in marriage and to the wearing of gowns by ministers.
- They asked for church administration to be 'according to Christ's own institution'. This vague phrase could be seen as an attack on the government of the Church by bishops.

At first James was inclined to be tactful and listen to the Puritans. He therefore called a conference between the bishops and the Puritans which he would preside over. Before the conference was held, at Hampton Court in 1604, more petitions had come in and James had become concerned about their tone and the methods used to stir up support. He saw the possibility of public disorder and his sympathy for the Puritans had largely gone before the conference met. The threat to the bishops particularly worried him. He saw the Church organisation as supporting him as supreme head of the Church and any attempt to undermine the bishops as a threat to his authority. As he said himself, 'No bishops, no king.'

The Puritans did not succeed in getting any of their demands for changes in ceremonies, but James did agree to

The title page of the Authorised Version of the Bible, 1611.

minor reforms. Bancroft, Archbishop of Canterbury 1604–11, followed up the defeat of the more extreme puritan demands with his canons (instructions) – see below – to enforce Church discipline.

The most important result of the Hampton Court Conference was a new translation of the Bible which eventually appeared in 1611: **the Authorised, or King James, Bible**, which was to survive as the Church of England's main Bible until the late twentieth century.

Despite the Puritans not getting the 'reforms' they wanted, James, like Elizabeth before him, was careful not to make life too difficult for them. The Church of England remained a 'broad church' in which different views could be accepted. When Bancroft died in 1611, he was replaced by George Abbott, a 'moderate', who was anxious not to stir up religious differences in the Church of England and could be seen as being, in some ways, a Puritan himself. James, therefore, did not have too many problems with Puritanism during his reign.

KEY TERM

The Authorised, or King James, version of the Bible. The 1611 Bible can be seen as one of the most important influences on the life and thought of the English people up to the twentieth century. It was read by all who could read, its superb language came to be quoted by everyone and the Anglican Church, whether Puritan-inclined or high church, looked to it for inspiration. Even today it is used among Anglicans; the more modern (perhaps more accurate) translations have never gained the status of the King James Bible, nor the affection that people still have for it.

Bancroft's canons. Archbishop Bancroft was determined to enforce some discipline in the Church. Using the Church Parliament 'Convocation', he issued 141 canons regulating many aspects of Church life. The canons were partly aimed at the more extreme puritan ministers who had never accepted all the rules of the Church of England. Included among the canons were instructions:

- On how ministers were to dress and conduct services. Ministers should wear a cape and gown. The congregation should kneel to receive communion.
- That ministers had to accept that the king was head of the Church of England.
- That the original 39 articles that had been the basis of the Elizabethan Church of England were correct.
- That ministers had to accept that the Prayer Book contained 'nothing contrary to the word of God'.

Most ministers accepted the ruling, but some extreme puritan ministers had doubts about parts of the Prayer Book and around 100 of them left the Church of England

Richard Bancroft, Archbishop of Canterbury 1604–11.

rather than agree to the canons. Bancroft also faced complaints in Parliament because MPs argued that Parliament, not convocation by itself, should settle Church matters. There were also disputes about the powers of Church courts. Bancroft was unpopular among the stronger Puritans, who had an easier life under his successor, Abbott.

The Puritans after the Hampton Court Conference. When Abbott became Archbishop of Canterbury in 1611 he was anxious to prevent more extreme Puritans leaving the Church and setting up independent congregations, as had happened in the 1590s when stronger Puritans had felt themselves under pressure. In East Anglia in particular, Independent congregations had gathered – called Brownists. They were named after their founder, Thomas Browne. During the early seventeenth century, many of the theology graduates (in religion) from Cambridge were strong Puritans, especially those from Emmanuel College. Abbott not only had sympathy for their views but also wanted them to become parish ministers within the Church of England. Therefore he did not try to make them agree to all the rules that Bancroft had laid down; for instance, he did not insist that gowns be worn. Also he did not discourage puritan lecturers. These were graduates in theology who had not found a post as parish ministers. Groups of puritan gentry and merchants employed these graduates to give them lectures on Sundays after church services. Later Archbishop Laud was to take away their licences to lecture as he saw them as a threat to the Church of England. While Abbott and King James were in control of the Church of England, it remained a tolerant church in which all but the most extreme Puritans could find a place.

James' caution with William Laud. In some ways Abbott was not a very dynamic archbishop, but this was probably an advantage because he did not look too closely into the beliefs of the ministers of the Church of England. James, although he had no love for the more extreme Puritans, was anxious that the Church should remain tolerant. This shows in the way he dealt with William Laud, who wanted to enforce his views on the Church and to exclude Puritans. Throughout his reign James refused to promote him. Therefore James was able to keep the Church of England from splitting into various groups with different ideas about Protestantism. It was to be a very different story under Charles, when Laud became archbishop.

KEY PEOPLE

Robert Catesby was a Catholic from a Warwickshire family. He opposed James' accession to the throne and was the organiser of the Gunpowder Plot. He left London after the plot to raise a revolt in Staffordshire but died fighting soon after.

The Gunpowder Plot 1605. The Catholics had hoped for more toleration from James. Like everyone else, they were expected to attend Anglican services on Sundays. If they did not, they were fined for recusancy. As James showed no sign of really wishing to change this, a small group of desperate, mainly young, Catholics, led by **Robert Catesby**, hired a cellar under the Houses of Parliament and

A contemporary engraving of the gunpowder plotters, including the names of the conspirators.

filled it with gunpowder, intending to blow up the House of Commons and the House of Lords when James was there. The man who was actually to light the fuse was **Guy Fawkes.** The plot was discovered, partly because one of the conspirators was reluctant to see one of his own relatives in the House of Lords blown up. He sent an anonymous letter, the conspiracy was uncovered and the plotters were rapidly arrested. Most Catholics were appalled by the plot, since they were, in the last resort, loyal to the king, despite their religion. James realised this and tried, unsuccessfully, to hold back the tide of anti-Catholic feeling that spread across the country. The event is still celebrated today on November the fifth – Bonfire Night.

KEY PEOPLE

Guy Fawkes was from Yorkshire and a fanatical Catholic. He was arrested after the plot was uncovered and put to death in February 1606.

It is certain that Robert Cecil knew something about the Gunpowder Plot before the letter was sent from one of the conspirators, Tresham, to his cousin, Lord Mounteagle, warning him to stay away from Parliament. This letter triggered the search of the cellars of the House of Commons. It is probable that Cecil was biding his time, hoping to catch all the conspirators.

Consequences of the plot. The king may, rightly, have seen the Gunpowder Plot conspirators as a group of desperate young men, untypical of English Catholics, but Parliament did not see the plot that way. In the 1606 session of Parliament the recusancy laws were tightened up and Catholics were required to take an oath of allegiance to James, which stated that the pope had no right to depose the king. The plot led to the confirmation of the anti-

Catholic feeling of the Protestant country gentry, both in Parliament and in the country at large.

FOREIGN POLICY 1604–24

KEY EVENT

The Treaty of London. Under the terms of the Treaty of London, Spain and England agreed to the following points:

- English merchants were allowed to trade with Spain and the important market of the Spanish Netherlands (modern Belgium).
- English merchants would not be arrested as heretics by the Spanish Inquisition.

The treaty was popular with the merchants, but Spain remained an object of suspicion among the country gentry in Parliament.

The Treaty of London 1604. When James came to the throne, England was at war with Spain. However, both England and Spain were tired of a war that was going nowhere. James, a natural peacemaker, was anxious to close it down. Elizabeth had supported the Dutch rebels fighting for their independence from Spain, but James had little sympathy for rebels against divine royal authority (as he saw it) and, in any case, the Dutch were not prepared to make peace with Spain. Therefore the Dutch were abandoned and James made a separate peace in the Treaty of London of 1604.

James' foreign policy objectives. James was anxious to maintain peace in Europe if he could but, compared to Spain and France, England was a 'middle rank' power: important but not vital. Both Spain and France were, in the modern sense, 'superpowers'; England was not in the same league so did not have as much influence as James thought.

The main problems in Europe

- Spain wished to regain control of the United Provinces (modern Holland), which had rebelled in the late sixteenth century. Although there was a truce between Spain and the United Provinces, it was clear that, when it felt strong enough, Spain would attempt to re-assert authority over the provinces.
- Europe was divided into Catholic and Protestant countries. The United Provinces, Sweden, Denmark and the north German states were Protestant. Both Spain and the Holy Roman Empire of Germany and Austria were ruled by the same Catholic family, the Hapsburgs, so Spain and Austria would be certain to act together. If they did, it would be to reconquer the United Provinces and to try to eliminate Protestantism from Europe.

The puritan-minded English country gentry were very suspicious of Spain and the Hapsburgs, seeing them as

European ambassadors at the Treaty of London negotiations in 1604.

representing the forces of the Counter-Reformation (anti-Protestantism) and absolutism.

- They tended to support the Dutch rebels and wanted England to side with, and support, the Protestant states.
- They looked back to the 'golden age' of Elizabeth I when England conducted a successful (and profitable) war against Spain, and figures such as Sir Francis Drake and Sir Walter Raleigh were the heroes of the country gentry.

James saw things differently:

- He hoped to balance the opposing forces in Europe in order to prevent a general European religious war.
- He did not share the prejudices against Spain and the Hapsburgs that the country gentry had but, on the other hand, he wanted to keep a 'balance of power'.

Therefore, from 1604 onwards he pursued a policy of friendship with Spain, while in 1608 he joined the Protestant Union of European States. He hoped to keep a foot in both camps to restrain both sides from reckless actions which could trigger a European religious war.

- In 1612 he married his daughter Elizabeth to Frederick, Elector Palatine, the leading German Protestant prince,

while maintaining a close relationship with Saramiento, the Spanish ambassador.
- By 1616 be was considering marrying Charles to the eldest daughter of the King of Spain – the *infanta*. This plan was much encouraged by the pro-Spanish Howard faction.

So anxious was he to maintain friendship with Spain that, in 1618, he had Sir Walter Raleigh executed after a failed expedition to find the 'city of gold' in South America. Sir Walter was an old enemy of the Spanish, and he had been in the Tower of London for years for his alleged part in a vague plot against James in 1604 – the 'Main Plot'. Released to find the city of gold, he clashed with the Spanish in South America and, on his return, was executed, much to the disgust of the country gentry and the public. A large crowd of Londoners gathered outside the Palace to protest at his execution and many saw it as

Sir Walter Raleigh, courtier, explorer and writer, c. 1552–1618.

being carried out at the urging of the hated Spanish ambassador.

The outbreak of the Thirty Years' War. In 1618 the long-expected European war broke out. The kingdom of Bohemia (the modern Czech Republic) had always had an elected king and the elected king had always been the Hapsburg Holy Roman Emperor. When Rudolph died, the new Emperor Ferdinand expected to be elected as a matter of formality. However, Ferdinand was not a tolerant, easy-going Catholic like Rudolph; he expected all his subjects in all his lands to be Catholics and he persecuted Protestants.

The Bohemians were Protestant and, fearing that Ferdinand would force them to be Catholics, they refused to elect him and offered the crown to Frederick, Elector Palatine. Frederick accepted but within eighteen months he had been driven from Bohemia at the Battle of the White Mountain, in 1620, by imperial (Hapsburg) troops. James had advised Frederick not to meddle in Bohemia, so he was not concerned about the result of the Battle of the White Mountain. However, it was the beginning of a general European war that was to be the **Thirty Years' War**, fought mainly in Germany between Catholic Hapsburgs and their allies and the German Protestant states, later joined by Sweden, Denmark and, eventually, France, which could not allow the Hapsburgs to win and dominate Europe. Despite the fact that the French were Catholics, power politics were more important than religion.

The problem of the Palatinate

- By the end of 1620 Frederick had lost not only his new kingdom of Bohemia but also his old kingdom of the Palatinate – a large German state on the Rhine – which had been invaded successfully by Spanish troops, despite being defended with great determination by English volunteers under Sir Horace Vere.
- James' attitude was that Frederick had no right to Bohemia but that he and James' daughter should keep their lands in Germany. James' status as king meant he had to support his son-in-law to regain the Palatinate, which James saw as Frederick's rightful land.

KEY EVENT

The Thirty Years' War 1618–48. There were four periods of war which together make up the Thirty Years' War:

- the Bohemian period 1618–25,
- the Danish period 1625–9,
- the Swedish period 1630–5,
- the Swedish–French period 1635–48.

During the first two periods the wars were mainly about religion. The latter two periods involved mainly political struggles against the Hapsburgs and Swedish wars of conquest.

KEY TERM

Spanish match. This plan involved marrying Charles to the Spanish *infanta*, daughter of the Spanish King Charles I.

KEY THEME

Terms of the Spanish match. They included toleration for Catholics in England, and the Spanish never promised to restore the Palatinate, which was one of the main reasons for the whole scheme.

The Spanish match. At first, James continued to pursue a policy of trying to persuade the Spanish to restore the Palatinate through the 'Spanish match', despite the aggressive attitude of the 1621 parliament towards Spain. In 1623 Charles and Buckingham travelled to Spain to try to arrange the marriage, a course of action that was very unpopular with the country gentry and the public. The expedition to Spain was very expensive, with gifts to Spanish courtiers and entertainment, and James seems to have disapproved of his son and Buckingham actually going to Spain, but by this time he was in failing health. Despite a long stay in Madrid, Charles failed to see the *infanta*, and the Spanish terms were too high for either Charles or Buckingham to accept. Charles and Buckingham felt humiliated by their treatment in Madrid and returned home determined on war with Spain. There was public rejoicing at the failure of the Spanish match, with bonfires and anti-Spanish/anti-Catholic sermons. For the first time, Buckingham was generally popular because of his new anti-Spanish policy and because of the general relief that the heir to the throne had not married a Spanish Catholic.

SUMMARY QUESTIONS

1 How did James and his parliaments clash up to 1611?

2 Why were James' finances such an important issue?

3 Why did the proposed union between Scotland and England fail?

4 How did James deal with the problem of the more extreme Puritans?

5 What were James' aims in foreign policy and how successful was he in achieving them?

6 'James I – For and Against': draw up a list of points arguing for him being a successful king, and a list of his shortcomings and failures.

CHAPTER 3

Charles I: the early years of the reign 1625–9

INTRODUCTION

Personality and character. Charles' personality was to have an important effect on the course of events over the next twenty-four years.

- **Divine right.** Like his father James, he was a believer in the divine right of kings. Unlike his father, he actually tried to put it into practice. Given his belief in the divine right of kings, he saw all Parliament's 'privileges', or rights, as being subject to the approval of the sovereign, not as liberties that had existed independently of the sovereign's wishes.
- **Criticism.** He saw all criticism, all discussion, as being potentially treacherous. He regarded anyone who questioned his actions as being disloyal.
- **Communication skills.** He was a poor communicator. His speeches in Parliament were brief and they often took the form of rebukes to Parliament, or statements of his views, with which he would allow no argument.
- **Henrietta Maria.** In some ways he was shy and tended to have only a small circle of 'friends' or courtiers. He was deeply attached to Buckingham until his assassination in 1628, then he turned his attention to his wife, Henrietta Maria, who had considerable influence over him. She was a strong 'absolutist', a French princess who was brought up in the continental belief that the monarch was all-powerful. She had no time at all for parliaments, or for the idea that subjects had 'liberties' which monarchs could not interfere with.
- **Religious views.** In religion he favoured the high-church **Arminian** group within the Church of England, because they stressed the divine nature of the monarch. Charles quickly promoted William Laud, the leading 'Arminian'; by 1628 he was Bishop of London. Even though James I

KEY THEME

The Arminians. This group believed that ceremonies, statues and bowing at the name of Jesus were vital parts of church services. They were hated by the Calvinist-minded puritan majority of the Church of England. To Puritans their services seemed like a return to the traditions of the Roman Catholic Church.

Arminians were named after a Dutch religious thinker called Arminius who had attacked some of the ideas behind Puritanism. Arminian came to be a general name given to those who wanted a high Church with ceremonies and who did not attack the Roman Catholic Church as strongly as most Protestants did.

A portrait of Charles I by the Dutch painter Van Dyck, c. 1638.

disliked Puritans, he had been too politically clever to promote high-church Arminians. James realised that Arminianism would cause deep offence to the majority of the puritan-minded Church of England. James said of Laud, 'He is a restless fellow and will never be satisfied until he brings things to a pitch of reformation floating in his own brain.' For Charles, however, Laud and those who thought like him were the monarch's natural supporters because they preached the divine right of kings, unlike some Puritan ministers who, he suspected, filled the minds of their congregations with 'subversive' ideas. For the majority of Charles' subjects Laudian ideas were a form of popery, of Roman Catholicism, taking over the Protestant Church of England, undermining it from within.

- **Charles and absolutism.** Absolutism was rule carried out by absolute monarchs. They ruled without parliaments, made all the laws and ruled as they wished. In modern terms they could be seen as dictators. Absolutism was gaining ground in seventeenth-century Europe: parliaments were being abolished by kings who wanted to centralise all power in their own hands. In the seventeenth century this was the modern monarchy and it seemed to be the way in which all countries would be ruled. So MPs in England became very worried that Charles had absolutist ideas and began to fear that Parliament's existence was threatened. As one MP said in 1626, 'We are the last parliament in Europe that retains its ancient privileges.'

The 'crisis of the 1620s'. Some historians, and some people who lived through the period 1624–9, saw it as one of a crisis. Sir Benjamin Rudyerd remarked in 1626, 'This is the crisis of parliaments by which we live or die.' In the 1660s Edward Hyde, Lord Clarendon, wrote his *History of the Great Rebellion*; when attempting to explain the causes of the Civil War he looked to 1625, with Charles' coming to the throne, for the starting point of his history.

During the period 1625–9, under the strain of raising troops and money for war with Spain and later France, Charles used methods that many thought illegal to force the country gentry to co-operate in raising troops that the counties paid for, while failing to gain a victory in Europe. The relationship between the Crown and the House of Commons suffered so much that by 1629 Charles was fed up with Parliament and Parliament was very suspicious of Charles' advisers, his methods and his policies.

KEY THEME

'Crisis of the 1620s' – the historical debate.

- Some historians have argued that there was a 'crisis' in the 1620s that did long-term damage to Charles' relations with his subjects. This was to be remembered in 1640 when the next crisis arose.
- Others argue that there was not a real crisis in the 1620s, just a series of temporary difficulties; they argue that the cause of the breakdown of 1640 was war with Scotland in 1637 (see later) and that the events of the 1620s had no long-term effects.

FOREIGN POLICY 1625–9

The main problem of the period for Charles was foreign policy. By 1625 Charles and Buckingham had attempted to set up an anti-Spanish 'front' to force the Hapsburgs to restore the Palatinate to Charles' brother-in-law. This was composed of:

- An alliance with Christian IV of Denmark whereby, in exchange for financial support from England, he would attack the Catholic Hapsburgs in north Germany.
- Financial support for the Dutch in the same cause.
- An English army of 6,000 men to be provided for the German Protestant mercenary commander, Ernst von Mansfeld, who had already fought for Frederick of the Palatinate.
- A sea war against Spain to try to cut off its supplies of gold and silver from South America. These supplies from the Spanish colonies were what paid for the forces of Spain and the Hapsburg emperor.

However, Parliament had voted subsidies worth only about £250,000 for sea war. They were not clear about the other plans that Charles and Buckingham had – plans that cost something in the region of £2 million. If all these plans had gone well, Parliament might have covered the costs, but they did not succeed and so Parliament was never prepared to meet the bill.

Failures. There was a series of foreign policy failures which were to make Charles and Buckingham unpopular. By 1626 the strategy was in ruins and Buckingham was being blamed for the failures.

KEY TERM

Impressment was when the JPs and Deputy Lieutenants in the counties simply forced people to go into military service.

- **Mansfeld's failure 1625.** The 6,000 troops were raised largely by **impressment**. They had no training and were equipped badly (at the counties' expense) before being shipped off to Flushing in Holland. Mansfeld did not have the organisation to feed or look after them and 4,000 died of disease and starvation, the rest never going into battle.
- **The Cadiz expedition 1625.** Charles and Buckingham decided to attack one of the main Spanish ports, Cadiz, to destroy as much of the Spanish fleet as they could and then to attack the Spanish treasure fleet as it came into range. Again, troops were raised from the counties, and most of them were untrained. They went ashore at Cadiz but then found a huge wine store. Discipline broke down and the troops had to be withdrawn to the ships having done nothing except capture, briefly, a small fort. Buckingham then decided to wait at sea for the Spanish fleet but never managed to intercept it.

There was not enough food on the ships for the troops and many of them had died by the time the pathetic remainder got back to Devon.
- **Christian IV.** Christian IV did invade north Germany but was soon decisively defeated by the imperial General Wallenstein.

The French match and alliance 1625. With the failure of the Spanish match in 1623 and Buckingham's new anti-Spanish policy, Charles and Buckingham looked for a new ally in Europe, and a new bride for Charles. **Henrietta Maria**, daughter of the King of France, was the choice. Although she was Roman Catholic, Charles and Buckingham could see some diplomatic advantages in the marriage. France, they thought, was becoming increasingly worried about the successes of the Hapsburg Spanish and

KEY PEOPLE

Christian IV was King of Denmark, Duke of Holstein and a leader of the Protestants. In August 1626 his forces were defeated at Luther am Barenberge.

Henrietta Maria was the wife of Charles I. She was an important figure at court. In the 1630s she encouraged dancing and balls at the palaces of Whitehall and Hampton Court. Most importantly, Henrietta Maria was a Roman Catholic. It was her Catholicism that upset Puritans and made them suspicious of Charles.

A portrait of Henrietta Maria by Van Dyck.

Imperialists in the Thirty Years' War, and might be persuaded to take part against them. Also Henrietta Maria would bring a dowry (wedding settlement) of £240,000, which would help Charles finance the war. The terms of the marriage agreement included toleration for Roman Catholics in England, which was to prove impossible to carry out and caused great suspicion in the country at large because, although the details of the agreement were secret, rumours had been circulating.

The break with France 1626–7. In order to please the French, Buckingham had lent them English ships, which were to be used against Protestant rebels (Huguenots) who were fighting the French Crown. The crews mutinied rather than fight fellow Protestants. Meanwhile Charles, anxious for parliamentary subsidies, wished to keep suspicions of secret 'Roman Catholic' deals with France to a minimum. He therefore did not carry out the part of the marriage treaty that dealt with giving Roman Catholics toleration. He also expelled most of Henrietta Maria's French Catholic servants. In these circumstances, relations between Charles and his new queen were cool, and she hated Buckingham as a rival for the king's affections.

Richelieu, the French chief minister, regarded Charles and Buckingham as unreliable and had no intention, at this stage, of joining them in a war against the Hapsburgs. Buckingham reversed his policy of trying to join in a French alliance and, to gain popularity (he hoped), decided to help the Huguenots, who were besieged by French royal forces in their stronghold, the port of La Rochelle.

War with two countries. So England found itself at war with the two most powerful nations in Europe at the same time, obviously a disastrous policy. In 1627 Buckingham led a naval expedition to try to land troops at La Rochelle to support the Huguenots. The landing at the Ile de Ré in 1627 was another military disaster and Buckingham had to retreat to his ships without helping the defenders of La Rochelle, who surrendered to the French royal forces shortly afterwards in 1628. By this time Buckingham was the most despised man in England, seen as the driving force behind a series of military failures, the Ile de Ré expedition being the last straw: 'Since England was England it received not so dishonourable a blow', said Sir Edwyn Sandys.

Buckingham's death. In 1628 Buckingham was preparing another expedition to help the Huguenots when he was assassinated by **John Felton**, a captain with a grudge against him from the last expedition. Charles never forgot or forgave the scenes of rejoicing in the House of Commons and he lost the heart for any further adventures in Europe, to support either the Protestant cause or his brother-in-law. By 1630/1 he had made peace with both France and Spain. During the 1630s he pursued a 'neutral' policy as far as any direct action was concerned, but favoured Spain.

KEY PERSON

John Felton had taken part in the military actions at Cadiz in 1625 and the Ile de Ré in 1627. He felt bitter against Buckingham because he had not been given promotion and he felt that he had been underpaid. Felton stabbed Buckingham in Portsmouth. He was hanged at Tyburn but became a popular hero.

The effect of the wars. The wars of the 1620s had put a lot of strain on the counties. Charles had to raise forced loans and the Deputy Lieutenants had to collect troops, who were fed and housed by the counties until they were transported to the ports, also at the counties' expense. Not only did this cause great upheaval and expense, but the troops were then thrown away in what the country saw as incompetent attacks. The effect of Charles and Buckingham's foreign policy was to cause real divisions between the Crown and the 'political nation', divisions that were to dominate the parliaments of the period 1625–9.

RELIGION

The rise of the Laudian 'Arminian' High-Church Party. Charles had always favoured this small group within the Church of England, and their promotion was rapid. On the day after the dissolution of the 1626 parliament, Charles issued a proclamation which seemed to support them and to attack the Puritan 'mainstream' of the Church of England.

Laudian ministers were active in preaching sermons supporting divine right and attacking Puritanism. In 1627, during the 'forced loan crisis', an Arminian minister, Sibthorpe, preached that to resist paying a forced loan to the king was against God's will because the king was God's representative on earth. This, to many, clearly showed the close relationship between the Arminians and royal 'absolutist' divine-right policies.

The downfall of Abbott. The puritan-minded Archbishop of Canterbury, George Abbott, had been in semi-retirement since 1621, not taking much part in church affairs since he had accidentally killed a gamekeeper with a crossbow while out hunting. Abbott had no love for the Arminians, and Sibthorpe's sermon seems to have been the trigger for him finally to start resisting their rise. Charles, naturally, found Sibthorpe's sermon very pleasing and he ordered it to be printed and published so that, as with other sermons, it would be read out in church services all over the country. Legally, the licence for printing sermons was issued by the archbishop, but he refused to license Sibthorpe's.

KEY PERSON

William Laud was distrusted by James but his religious ideas were similar to those of Charles. In 1627 he was made Bishop of Bath and Wells before becoming Bishop of London two years later. In 1633, he was made Archbishop of Canterbury, a post he held until he was executed in 1645.

Laud's aims were as follows:

- He wanted to return the Church of England to a more powerful position.
- He wanted to suppress Puritanism and Puritan preachers.
- He tried to improve the financial position of the clergy.

Charles' reply was to suspend Abbott, taking away all his powers. **William Laud** was made Bishop of London, and became very influential within the Church of England by 1628. He used his influence to promote Arminians and attack Calvinist puritan ministers, and he tried to introduce high-church practices in church services. By 1628 there was serious concern about the apparent undermining of the Protestant nature of the Church of England, as the high-church Laudians were seen as secret Roman Catholics, or Roman Catholic sympathisers. Buckingham's apparent support for them only increased their general dislike.

EVENTS 1625–9

The parliament of 1625

The first parliament of Charles' reign met in an atmosphere of gloom. There was a severe outbreak of the plague which killed about 20 per cent of the population of London, Norwich and Exeter. The parliament even had to move to Oxford to avoid it.

Tonnage and poundage. From the beginning there were suspicions of a 'soft' policy towards Roman Catholics.

Charles opening Parliament in 1625.

At the same time, Sir Robert Phelips and Sir Edward Coke decided to attack Buckingham politically. As Lord Admiral he was responsible for the navy, and pirates were preying on English shipping off the west coast. The issue they chose to attack Buckingham on was **tonnage and poundage**. In theory the money raised from this tax was for 'protection of the seas' and Buckingham seemed to be failing in his duty in this respect. Phelips and Coke persuaded the House of Commons to vote tonnage and poundage for one year only. It seems that this was intended not as a direct challenge to the Crown by

KEY TERM

Tonnage and poundage. A form of customs duty, tonnage and poundage was normally voted in by the first parliament of a new reign for the life of the monarch, who would therefore collect it automatically after the first 'grant'.

Parliament, but simply as a concrete way of protesting about the Duke of Buckingham. Charles saw it as a direct challenge, ignored the Commons and simply continued to collect tonnage and poundage.

Charles' discontent with Parliament. The Commons were not convinced that a land war was necessary and voted only two subsidies for a sea war. One royal supporter in the Commons warned that if Parliament would not pay for the war it was being disloyal and unrealistic; he said that 'some new way' must be found. With Buckingham under attack in the House of Commons, with speeches being made asserting that there was going to be toleration for Roman Catholics and with no real financial support from the Commons, Charles decided to dismiss Parliament. Between the 1625 and 1626 parliaments the situation got worse.

KEY THEME

Resentment against Buckingham. In 1624 Buckingham had already angered the great East India Company by arranging for them to be fined £10,000 by James for attacking a Portuguese fort at Ormuz, but this was after he had extracted £10,000 from them in exchange for a promise not to bring the matter to the king's attention. His expeditions had involved taking over ships from the Levant and East India companies, which had hit their profits.

Buckingham removes his enemies. Buckingham strengthened his position at court and his hold over the king by 'purging' the court of any who were not his wholehearted supporters (people who owed their careers to him). Bristol, who had been ambassador in Spain at the time of the Spanish match, found himself under pressure. Lord Keeper Williams, an enemy of Buckingham's (whom James had protected), was dismissed and the Earl of Arundel was arrested. Even in the counties, lords, lieutenants and their deputies were purged (removed from office) if they were not Buckingham 'clients'. A gap began to widen between the 'court' and the 'country' – the 'country' seeing Buckingham as the power behind the throne, manipulating everything.

The failure of the City merchants to lend to Charles. Charles was desperate for money. An attempt to raise a loan in the City of London failed. The Crown's credit with the City merchants was exhausted.

Disillusion with the war. The effect of the failure of the Cadiz expedition in 1625 was widespread. Sir John Eliot, a Buckingham 'client', turned against the favourite when he saw the pathetic survivors arriving back in Devon. A minister in Dorset preached that God was punishing England with defeat, because the land was 'not governed by justice, but by bribery and extortion'. The total failure of Mansfeld's expedition as well only increased concern and anger.

The parliament of 1626

Tension between king and Commons. There were many reasons for tension between the king and Parliament. The **situation in the country** was not good and there were immediate reasons for friction. However, Charles still needed money in 1626 and therefore he called another parliament.

- To avoid attacks on Buckingham, some of his leading opponents, such as Sir Edward Coke and Sir Robert Phelips, were appointed sheriffs before the election, which prevented them standing as MPs. However, Parliament was in no mood to co-operate when it met.
- Parliament's discontent was worsened by a sermon preached by Laud at the opening of Parliament. In his sermon Laud seemed to support divine right: 'A royal command must be God's glory, and obedience to it a subject's honour.'

Attack on Buckingham. The attack on Buckingham quickly followed the opening of Parliament. The MP **Sir John Eliot** said, 'Our honour is ruined, our ships are sunk, our men perished, not by the enemy . . . but by those we trust.' The attack on the royal favourite was not confined to the Commons. The Lords decided to support Arundel and Bristol, the peers whom Buckingham had attacked previously. The king was petitioned to release Arundel. However, Bristol was a different case. Because he was ambassador to Spain in 1623 he knew some very disturbing details of Charles' and Buckingham's negotiations with the Spanish in that year. Most damaging was the information that in attempting to persuade the Spanish court to agree to the marriage, large bribes had been given out to Spanish courtiers. Even worse, Charles had made promises with regard to the position of Roman Catholics in England. In 1626 Bristol threatened to make it all public.

To keep Bristol quiet, Charles had him charged with treason. Bristol replied in the House of Lords with a charge

KEY THEME

Situation in the country in 1626. War with Spain had affected English cloth exports and there was a very bad harvest in 1625. This created widespread unrest and many MPs reflected the pessimistic mood.

KEY PERSON

Sir John Eliot was a loyal member of the court. However, he was shocked by the incompetence of the Cadiz expedition. As a result he became an opponent of the king in Parliament. After his speech in 1626 he was imprisoned. In 1627 he refused to contribute to the forced loan and was imprisoned again. In 1629 he drew up the Three Resolutions of the Commons. As a result he was sent to the Tower, where he died in 1632.

of treason against Buckingham, giving out a lot of very damaging evidence in support of this, and the Lords accepted the charge against Buckingham.

Charles dismisses Parliament. Charles was worried and threatened Parliament with the warning, 'Remember that parliaments are altogether in my power for their calling, sitting and dissolution.' However, despite his threat, the Commons voted to impeach (try) Buckingham. The fact that the Commons and the Lords (who usually supported the Crown) were in alliance against Buckingham spelt real danger for the favourite, and Charles had no option but to dismiss Parliament without any of the hoped-for financial support.

Finance without Parliament 1626–8

Charles' financial problems. Charles' European military commitments made his financial position desperate.

- He had sold £350,000 worth of Crown land to the City of London merchants and financiers by the end of 1627, partly to pay off his debts.
- Rents from Crown lands had been an important part of royal revenue in 1603; now there was little left.

Charles was, therefore, storing up problems for the future as the Crown was made poorer in the long term.

Courtiers had already warned that if Parliament would not grant enough subsidies to pay for the war, the king would be forced to find other ways of raising money. After dissolving the 1626 parliament Charles first tried a **benevolence**. Very few were willing to pay.

KEY TERM

Benevolence was an attempt to persuade those tax payers who would have paid a parliamentary subsidy to give him the money.

The forced loan of 1627. Having failed to persuade the country to provide the funds that were needed, Charles decided on more forceful methods. All those who normally paid parliamentary subsidies were pressured by 'commissioners' to 'lend'. Faced with direct royal commands to pay, few were prepared to refuse. However, the forced loan was opposed on legal grounds. Lord Chief Justice Crew was dismissed for refusing to state that the loan was legal, and some 'refusers' were arrested and imprisoned.

The Five Knights' case 1627. Five gentlemen who had been imprisoned for refusing to contribute tried to test the legality of their imprisonment. They applied for a writ of **habeas corpus.** If they were tried then the whole legality of forced loans would be tested in a court of law. The Attorney General (the royal legal officer), Sir Robert Heath, argued that the Crown must have emergency powers of arrest. The judges agreed but their judgement was not clearly in Charles' favour; Heath tried to change the records of the court to make Charles' actions completely secure as far as future arrests were concerned. This was done at Charles' 'request' and when the story came out it did considerable damage to Charles' reputation. The Five Knights were released at the beginning of 1628, but the legality of forced loans was to concern the 1628 parliament.

KEY TERM

Habeas corpus. This was an application to the judges of the King's Bench to be tried for an offence (if it was an offence) or be released. As it stood, the Five Knights were being imprisoned without trial or accusation of a crime.

Billeting and martial law. Approximately 50,000 troops had been raised between 1625 and 1627. The responsibility for raising them lay with the Deputy Lieutenants for each county. These troops were 'billeted' on the local population, which found itself having to pay for their food as well as being forced to have them living in their homes. In some cases, those who had been slow in paying forced loans found troops billeted with them. Many of the troops were completely undisciplined and committed crimes in the localities where they were billeted. Some areas protested about the behaviour of troops and the cost and injustice of billeting. The Deputy Lieutenants often found themselves arguing with the local Justices of the Peace, especially as, in order to have some control over the troops, **martial law** (military law) was declared in areas where they were billeted.

KEY TERM

Martial law replaced ordinary law and the ordinary legal rights of subjects. This was very disturbing to the legally minded country gentry, who saw martial law as a form of dictatorship.

Increasing discontent with Charles. Had Charles' and Buckingham's military expeditions been successful, local anger might have died down, but given the failures from Cadiz to the Ile de Ré, by 1628 the country was in a state of outrage. Some of the Deputy Lieutenants, who were the leading gentry in their counties, began to lose heart at the unpopularity they had created for themselves among their gentry friends and neighbours, by following royal policies. Unlike courtiers, they had to live in their counties. The Deputy Lieutenants in the Isle of Wight described the situation as 'intolerable'.

The 1628 parliament

The parliament met in a mood of distrust.

- Buckingham was now the most hated man in England, with his control of court patronage and his failed foreign policy.
- The king had aroused suspicions with regard to his religious views because of his promotion of Arminians.
- Martial law and billeting were seen as illegal and against the subject's rights.
- The king's conduct in the Five Knights case gave MPs cause for concern; he seemed to have little regard for the law. Sir John Eliot remarked, 'Where is Law? Where is property? It is fallen into the chaos of a higher power.'

Why did Charles call Parliament? Charles had called Parliament not because he believed his martial law, billeting and forced loans policies were wrong and that he should give them up and co-operate with Parliament to gain subsidies in the 'old accepted way', but because he still needed about half a million pounds and only Parliament could provide that sort of money.

Parliament's response. Parliament, on the other hand, deeply disturbed by the apparent inability of the king to understand the constitution as they understood it, and concerned about attacks on the rights of the subject, were determined to get Charles to accept that there were limits to his powers.

The Petition of Right 1628. Sir Edward Coke, the great champion of the common law and the constitution, decided on a Petition of Right that would define the traditional rights of the subject which had existed 'time out of mind'. **John Pym**, who was to be prominent for the first time in this parliament, argued that the aim of petition was not to give Parliament more power and the king less, but rather that they were 'demanding their ancient and due liberties, not suing [demanding or requesting] for any new'. The petition started with a list of supposed illegal acts committed by royal government in the past years, then laid out that:

KEY PERSON

John Pym was to become the leading parliamentary opponent of the Stuarts. In the 1620s he was a leading figure in the impeachment of Buckingham and in putting forward the Petition of Right. He was a strong opponent of Laud.

- Forced loans were illegal.
- No free man should be imprisoned without 'just cause shown'.
- Soldiers should not be billeted on private individuals against their will.
- Martial law was illegal.

The petition, if signed by the king, would become part of the legal constitution and, at first, he was reluctant to sign. This reluctance only aroused further suspicion among MPs. Eventually Charles agreed to sign it. The passing of the petition on 8 June was a national event with bonfires lit in London and other cities.

Continuing attacks on Charles. The passing of the petition, followed by the Commons voting five subsidies (about £280,000), did not really calm the atmosphere of crisis. It was discovered that Charles had attempted to raise professional cavalry from Germany in early 1628 and some members believed that Buckingham intended to use them for a military coup, to set up a 'continental style' absolutist government backed by a professional army.

Also, Charles' religious policies came under attack; the Commons impeached a Laudian minister, Manwaring, who had been prominent in preaching in favour of forced loans.

The Commons voted for two 'remonstrances' (petitions) to the king:

- One demanded that the recusancy laws against Catholics be enforced and complained about the favouritism shown to Arminian over Calvinist ministers, and also about the excessive power of the Duke of Buckingham.
- The second complained about the continued collection of tonnage and poundage, which had not been voted in Parliament.

The effects of the death of the Duke of Buckingham 1628. Between the sessions of Parliament, Buckingham was assassinated. However terrible the murder was for Charles, in some ways it created a different situation.

- Anglo-French relations improved as Charles drew closer to Henrietta Maria.
- Some MPs, who saw Buckingham as the 'evil councillor' who had led Charles astray, now felt that they could support the Crown. Now the 'Grievance of Grievances' (as Sir Edward Coke had described the duke) was removed, there seemed to be a possibility of a new relationship between Charles and the political nation.

One of the leading parliamentarians who now found that – with the Petition of Right apparently having settled the constitutional arguments, and the Duke of Buckingham dead – a new relationship could emerge was **Thomas Wentworth,** who accepted the post of President of the Council of the North. Wentworth, later Earl of Strafford, was to become one of Charles' chief ministers in the 1630s.

KEY PERSON

Thomas Wentworth had been one of those who opposed certain aspects of Charles' rule. In 1627 he was put into prison for refusing to pay the forced loan. However, his ambition led him to change sides in 1628 and accept the position of President of the Council of the North. This position gave him the power to rule in the king's name the section of England located north of the Trent.

Further problems in 1629

When Parliament re-assembled on 20 January 1629, two issues were, for many MPs, still to be settled. One was religion, the other tonnage and poundage.

- **Religion.** The king had promoted the leading Arminian, Montague, to be Bishop of Chichester so there seemed no chance of his accepting the view of the puritan-minded MPs that Arminianism was a threat to the Protestant Church of England.
- **Tonnage and poundage.** Some merchants had refused to pay tonnage and poundage, and had had their goods confiscated. One of these, John Rolle, was an MP and the Commons took up his case. At first the attack was on the hated customs farmers, which would avoid a direct challenge to the king.

On the question of tonnage and poundage, Charles took the line that, because of the emergency caused by war, he was entitled to carry on collecting these customs. The Commons were not united, nor were they clear whether to attack the Arminians in the Church of England, or the king's collection of tonnage and poundage. The debates became confused, with Eliot finding a new 'evil councillor' in the Lord Treasurer Weston, who was a secret Roman Catholic.

The Three Resolutions 1629. Eliot and his group became convinced that the king intended to dismiss Parliament and rule without it, so when the king declared another adjournment on 2 March, the Eliot group barred the door and held the Speaker down in his chair while they passed the Three Resolutions:

- That anyone bringing in popery or Arminianism should be 'accounted a capital enemy of the king and kingdom'.
- That anyone who should advise the king to collect tonnage and poundage was also a 'capital enemy'.
- That anyone who should pay tonnage and poundage under these circumstances was a 'capital enemy'.

Eliot and his group had 'overstepped the mark' for some MPs, and when Charles imprisoned him and some of his supporters, and dismissed Parliament, some MPs who shared a lot of Eliot's fears still thought that he had gone too far.

Charles dismisses Parliament. The incident of the Three Resolutions confirmed Charles in his view that the House of Commons would not co-operate with him and that he could rule more effectively without having to 'compromise' his royal dignity by trying to come to agreements with the House. Personal Rule, without Parliament, was the obvious alternative given his attachment to divine right and his support for a religious policy which the majority of the House of Commons would not accept. On 10 March 1629 Charles dissolved Parliament.

KEY THEME

Parliamentary reactions to Eliot. Sir Simonds D'Ewes, the puritan diarist of the House of Commons, had very grave misgivings about Charles' policies, but at the same time he thought Eliot irresponsible and wrote, 'Divers [several] fiery spirits in the House of Commons were very faulty and cannot be excused.'

SUMMARY QUESTIONS

1 How was Charles different from his father in his beliefs, character and attitudes?

2 Why was the Duke of Buckingham so unpopular?

3 Why have some historians seen the period 1625–9 as 'the crisis of the 1620s'?

4 Why, by 1629, had Charles decided to rule without Parliament?

CHAPTER 4

Personal Rule 1629–40

INTRODUCTION

In 1629 Charles I dismissed Parliament and 'forbade' people to speak of calling another. Parliament did not meet again until May 1640 and was called only because of the Scottish crisis.

There has been considerable debate about Charles' intentions in this period. Did he want to set up some form of continental-style absolutism, or did he merely wish to rule without Parliament because he had found parliaments troublesome during the 1620s?

KEY TERM

Personal Rule. The period between 1629 and 1640 was known as a period of Personal Rule. This was because during that period Charles ruled without consulting Parliament. Some called it the 'eleven years' tyranny'.

Main points about Personal Rule

- **Eleven years.** Personal Rule was distinguished by several factors from other periods when Parliament did not meet. The first of these was the length of time – eleven years – although James had gone eleven years with only a very brief parliament in 1614 (the Addled Parliament). There had been frequent, almost annual, parliaments in the 1620s, and even during Elizabeth's reign parliaments had met regularly.
- **Sources of finance.** Charles was obliged to look for new sources of finance in the absence of parliamentary subsidies. The new revenue-raising schemes seemed to indicate that he was prepared to ride roughshod over the 'rights' of his subjects; they were also perceived to be a threat to property.
- **Religion during Personal Rule.** The religious policies of Charles and Archbishop Laud were destructive of the 'broad church' that Elizabeth had created and James had maintained. Many Puritans saw Laud as a secret Catholic.
- **Foreign policy.** Foreign policy during Personal Rule was basically English neutrality but a neutrality that favoured Spain.

The anti-court consensus. In the minds of the 'political nation', the combination of these four elements of Personal Rule led to the strong suspicion that there was a conspiracy to undermine the Protestant religion in order to set up a Catholic absolutism. This fear was to be the driving force behind the 'anti-court consensus' of 1640. Charles did nothing to calm these fears, largely because:

- He was a shy non-communicative man, unable to reach out to his subjects in the way that Elizabeth, or even James, had done.
- Given his belief in divine right, he saw no reason to compromise or to explain his policies. Subjects were to obey; he was God's representative on earth.

RELIGION DURING PERSONAL RULE

Laudian dominance. Archbishop Laud was virtually in charge of the Church by 1628, as Abbott had been suspended following his refusal to license sermons praising divine right. On the death of Abbott in 1633, Laud became Archbishop of Canterbury. As soon as bishops died, they were replaced by Laudians who were determined to enforce high-church Laudian practices. By 1640 there were very few bishops who were not Laudians appointed by Laud. Laudian bishops did not behave as previous bishops had. They were determined to enforce what they saw as their rights and took no notice of the views of the gentry and the people who lived in their **dioceses**. Bishops such as Bishop Wren, first of Norwich and then of Ely diocese, and Bishop Montague of Chichester came to be hated by many in their dioceses for their ruthless determination to enforce Laudian ideas.

KEY TERM

A **diocese** is an area of Church organisation. Every bishop controls a diocese.

Laud's aims. Laud's policies can be seen on several levels.

- He wanted to restore the 'beauty of holiness' to church services. To him, ceremonies and the position of the altar were a vital part of worship.
- He also wanted to restore to the Church the wide power and influence that it had held in politics and society before the Reformation.

William Laud, Archbishop of Canterbury 1633–45.

- He was concerned to raise the educational level of the parish clergy and to make them the 'equal of any gentleman in England'.

The altar question. Many churches had a communion table in the middle of the church, this being seen as the Protestant way of doing things. The 'altar' at the east end of the church, separate from the congregation, was seen by many as a symbol of the Roman Catholic attitude to communion. The communion table was not always respected. It was reported that in some parishes the congregation left their hats on the table. Laud, who was determined that the altar should be a special place, ordered that the communion table, or altar as he called it, should

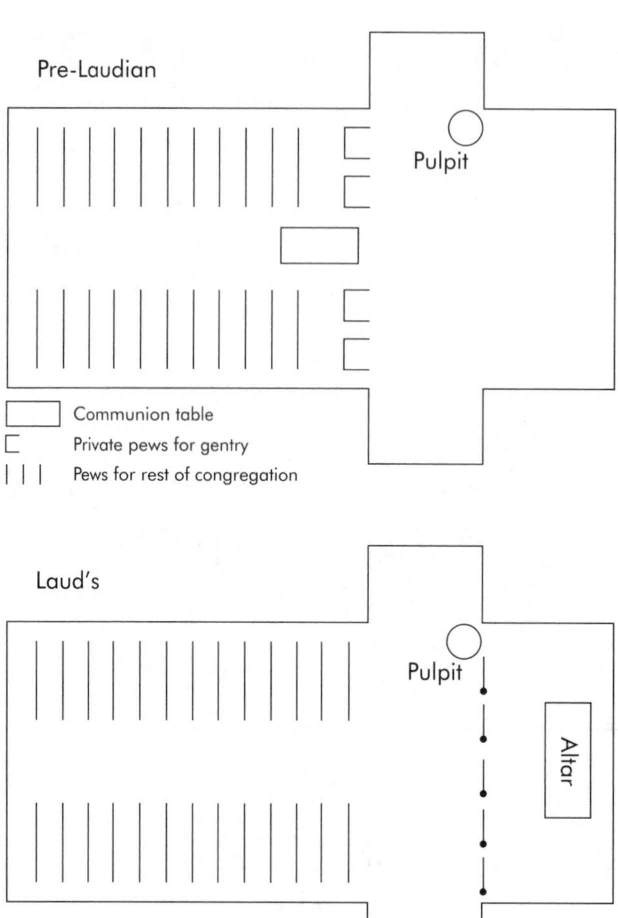

Pre- and post-Laud church layouts.

be removed to the east end of the church and railed off. Only the minister should approach it. Thus in some ways Laud can be seen as a reformer, but for the puritan-minded this instruction was seen as another sign that Laud was in sympathy with Roman Catholic ideas.

Reasons for opposition to Laud. Laud provoked opposition among a wide range of people who objected to and feared his policies, not only on religious grounds but also on political and social grounds. Many of the gentry who were not particularly strongly puritan still found themselves opposing Laud because of his use of power in the Royal Council and the attitude of Laudian clergy towards the gentry.

- **Laud's belief in divine right.** Laud believed in divine right, and associated himself fully with Charles' policies

KEY THEME

Reasons for Laud's policies. There were good reasons for Laud's policies. His concern for the 'beauty of holiness' did not just cover ritual in church, but the state of church buildings themselves.

- Many churches were in poor condition and Laud was anxious, in modern terms, to restore them.
- Many of the clergy were ill-educated and deferred to the local gentry.
- Laud's 'railing off of altars' can be seen not only as an indication of his belief in the importance of the communion service, but as an attempt to bring decency and respect to the altar. There had been cases of dogs urinating against the communion table, and in one church in Suffolk a dog had even run away with the communion bread in its mouth.

It was Laud's lack of tact that did much to destroy the good that he wanted to do.

KEY TERM

Cardinal is the highest rank a Roman Catholic priest can achieve apart from becoming Pope.

in the 1630s. His policies aroused opposition among much of the population. Laudian churchmen preached sermons supporting divine right and absolute obedience to the royal will. Thus everything that Laud did had a political aspect.

- **Laud's choice of religious ceremonies.** His views on religious ceremonies, vestments (the priest's clothes), bowing at the name of Jesus and beautifying churches ran up against very deep-rooted prejudices, or attitudes, among Puritans. The Laudian high-church service was visibly different from the 'mainstream' puritan-influenced services that many had come to regard as being the 'English Protestant way'. For many, the ceremonies were an obvious return to Roman Catholic services. The ritual of the Laudian Church seemed to be the same as that of the Roman Catholic Church and the Laudians were suspected of being secret papists.
- **Laud and Roman Catholicism.** Laud was not a Roman Catholic; he simply did not share the prejudice held by most English people towards the Roman Catholic Church. However, even the pope thought that Laud's church policies seemed to indicate that the English Church was moving back towards Rome. He had offered Laud the post of **Cardinal** in 1634. Laud refused, but the way he phrased his refusal would not have been strong enough for the Puritans as he said he could not accept 'with Rome as it is'. This would have been regarded by many as a very weak denunciation of the Roman Catholic Church.
- **Laud's aim to raise the status of the clergy.** Laud was also determined to raise the status of the parish priest and make him independent of the local gentry. The gentry were used to the parish priest being a respectful figure, following their wishes with regard to services and not attempting to interfere with their authority in the parish. Laud's aim, to raise the status of the clergy to 'equal to any gentleman in England', was much resented. The gentry often constructed their own private family pews in their local churches, which showed their status in the community, setting them apart from their tenants and the 'lower orders' in the congregation. Laud ordered these pews to be removed. The gentry felt they had been humiliated in their own private area and shown up in front of their tenants and the lower orders.

- **Laud's background.** Laud did not appear to respect the social system; the only authority he emphasised was that of the king. He was a 'self-made man', the son of a clothier, and his two strongest allies among the bishops, Wren and Neile, were also from humble origins. They all showed no respect for rank and dignity. Laud insulted and bullied the gentry in **Star Chamber** and **High Commission.** They were not used to being spoken to in this way by clergymen – even archbishops should know their place. William Prynne referred to 'lordly prelates [bishops] raised from the dunghill'. The 'lordly' was, of course, a play on words referring to Laud.

Therefore, Laud was seen as undermining not only the Protestant nature of the Church of England, but the social structure as well. He raised very strong feelings among the puritan gentry. A puritan gentleman, Sir Harbottle Grimston, called him 'that pestilential stye of all filth'. To some extent Laud had only himself to blame. He did not try to persuade the gentry to co-operate in his reforms and he was not a compromiser – 'he will break ere he bend' observed a contemporary. He saw all opponents as obstacles to be crushed, not to be 'won over' by persuasion.

The famous case of Burton, Prynne and Bastwick 1637. This case illustrates both Laud's indifference to 'public opinion' and his determination to show the power of the Church. The three gentlemen were punished for libels against the bishops, but although they were gentlemen they were treated like common criminals, having their ears clipped and standing in the **pillory**. If this punishment was meant to silence opposition to Laud's policies, it backfired. A vast crowd spread flowers in their path and dipped their handkerchiefs in the blood from their severed ears; they were generally regarded as martyrs for the 'Protestant puritan' cause. Also the punishment of gentlemen in this way was seen by the gentry as a threat to their social position; as Prynne warned in the pillory, 'look to yourselves gentlemen, for you will be next'. Laud's policies, therefore, were creating opposition not only on account of Puritanism but because these were Puritan gentlemen whom their fellow gentry would not have expected to be humiliated in this way.

KEY TERMS

Star Chamber and High Commission. These courts were both part of the legal system. Star Chamber was a royal court without a jury, in which members of the Royal Council sat. The High Commission was a royal court that was also the highest Church court.

KEY PEOPLE

Henry Burton, William Prynne and John Bastwick. William Prynne was a puritan writer of pamphlets – a pamphleteer. In his pamphlets he attacked what he saw as the excesses of Laud's Church. In 1633 he published an attack on the theatre. He was imprisoned, pilloried and had his ears cropped. In response he wrote a series of pamphlets with **Burton** and **Bastwick** attacking Laud.

KEY TERM

Pillory. In the seventeenth century, lower-class criminals were put in the pillory, which was a wooden block that trapped their neck and hands. The public could then, if they wished, throw stones or vegetables at them. Gentry were never put in the pillory until Laud humiliated Burton, Prynne and Bastwick in 1637.

KEY THEME

Effects of Laud's policies. Perhaps the major source of problems was Laud's determination to have uniformity of services and ceremonies in an English Protestant Church that had survived by being a 'broad church' in which the various views could be accommodated.

In trying to push the Church in a high-church direction, regardless of the feelings and prejudices of a large puritan-minded section of the population, he created an opposition that was to find its voice in 1640, and to almost destroy the Anglican Church.

His desire for uniformity was to create another disaster in his dealings with the Scottish Church and to lead directly to the downfall of Personal Rule.

Laud's influence. The belief grew that Laud was a secret Roman Catholic subverting the Church and the order of society, and supporting absolutist policies in the state. The appointment of the Bishop of London, Juxon, as Lord Treasurer in 1636 was hailed by Laud – 'no churchman has had it since Cardinal Wolsey's time' (the 1520s). Laud sat in every royal court as well as Church courts such as High Commission. He even sat on the Commission for Enclosure, fining gentry who had enclosed common land. Star Chamber, the royal court, was disliked and Laud used Star Chamber to punish his political enemies. He also made sure that the powers of Church courts all over the country were used to the full. Archbishop Abbott and the Elizabethan archbishops had tended to let the power of Church courts die. Laud was determined to reinforce them. The appointment of a bishop, Juxon, as Lord Treasurer in 1636 was seen as another sign that the Church was taking over the machinery of government.

The 'Book of Sports' 1633. The Puritans objected to most activities on Sundays, except Bible reading and attendance at church services or lectures by puritan lecturers. Laud re-issued the *Book of Sports* in 1633, encouraging dancing, archery and other activities on Sundays after church services. Some rural communities probably welcomed these, others were outraged.

Lecturing. There was an 'overproduction' of theology (religion) graduates from the universities of Oxford and Cambridge. Some of them could not find a post as a parish minister. They became 'lecturers', being paid to give lectures to puritan-minded groups after 'official' church on Sunday. Laud was suspicious of lecturers because he suspected their ideas of being too puritan and possibly subversive. He decided to tighten up on what he called 'The Ratsbane of Lecturing' and took away licences from lecturers. Many groups who had 'subscribed' to the salary of a lecturer were outraged.

FINANCIAL POLICIES

Charles' dilemma. Although the value of parliamentary subsidies had been going down, Charles' decision to rule without Parliament created a potential financial problem for him.

- Obviously war could not be continued without parliamentary subsidies – it was simply too expensive – so he lost no time in making peace with both France, in 1630, and Spain, in 1631.
- He did, however, need to maintain the royal household, live like a king and indulge his tastes, especially in art collecting, so it was necessary to get the most out of all the potential sources of revenue at his disposal. In order to do this, Charles pushed his legal rights to the limits and revived long forgotten royal revenue-raising devices. They kept him solvent but aroused great resentment.

Charles raised money in the following ways.

- **Forest fines.** The boundaries of the royal forests were declared to be those of Edward III's reign. People living in areas that had been royal forest – in the distant past – were fined, even though they had no idea that where they lived had once belonged to the king. Half of Essex was declared royal forest, and Rockingham Forest in Northamptonshire was increased from 6 to 60 square miles. The biggest fine was on the Earl of Salisbury, who was fined £20,000 for 'encroaching' on royal forest, but many other landowners were fined smaller sums.
- **Distraint of knighthoods.** James I's policy of selling knighthoods had made the honour unattractive but Charles found a way of still making money from honours without selling them. Those who had refused knighthoods were fined for **distraint of knighthood**. This caused great offence because knighthoods had been sold for £30 under James and many country gentry regarded the honour as not worth having.
- **Nuisances.** London grew rapidly in this period. In theory there should have been no building outside London's city walls. In practice this had been ignored; many people had built houses outside the walls without

KEY TERM

Distraint of knighthood was refusal to accept the honour of knighthood from the king, and thus insulting him.

any control. Those who had done this were forced to buy a licence to 'commit a nuisance' – or, in other words, to pay for planning permission after the event.

- **Monopolies.** These reappeared in different forms, one of the most resented being the soap monopoly, which actually led to a rather modern public test in 1634: clothes were washed in monopolists' soap and 'free enterprise' soap to see which one 'washed whiter'. The monopolists' soap appears to have failed the test but the public still had to buy it. Other monopolies reappeared, despite the Monopolies Act of 1624, and aroused as much resentment as previous monopolies had done.
- **Plantations.** In 1632 the City of London was fined for failing to push forward the plantation of Ulster. It should have found Protestant families to take over land in Ireland.
- **Customs farmers.** The hated customs farmers gave the Crown a larger sum in exchange for the right to collect the customs but, of course, passed on the costs to the merchants.
- **The Court of Wards.** The much disliked Court of Wards doubled its income in this period to £76,000.

Ship money. The one tax that probably caused strongest opposition was ship money. In theory coastal counties were required to provide ships for royal service in times of emergency, almost always in wartime. In practice coastal counties charged most inhabitants a rate and sent money rather than ships. The JPs normally set and collected the rate. In 1634 sheriffs were required to collect ship money even though England was not at war. The money was said to be needed to protect coastal shipping against pirates. In 1635 ship money was required from all counties on the basis that the 'charge of defence which concerneth all men ought to be supported by all'. Every year from 1634 to 1640 ship money was collected, in the first three years raising about £190,000 a year, all of which was spent on the navy.

However, the tax raised several issues:

- Firstly, it was new to the inland counties.
- Secondly, it became a permanent tax, not an emergency tax, and seemed to become part of the regular royal income.

'The Sovereign of the Seas', a warship built with ship money.

- Thirdly, the navy was seen to be used not to protect against piracy, but to help to convoy Spanish ships.
- Fourthly, nearly everyone paid it.

Hampden's case. The constitutional issue came to a head in **Hampden's case** in 1637. John Hampden, a Buckinghamshire gentleman, refused to pay ship money. Because sheriffs had experienced some difficulties with collection, it became a test case. The argument revolved around whether the king had the right to declare an emergency and then tax his subjects. In theory he had, but by making it a permanent tax he had weakened the argument that there was an emergency. The problem was, if the king was not to judge when there was an emergency, who should? If it were found that the king did not have the right to decide when there was an emergency, this would take away one of his constitutional rights over foreign policy and defence. In the event, the judges decided seven to five in favour of the king. The fact that five judges, all royal appointments, decided against the Crown was seen as significant and took the gloss off the king's victory.

The successes and failures of Charles' financial policies. Charles' financial policies in the 1630s certainly caused resentment, not just because people do not like to pay taxes, but because of the high-handed and legally dubious methods

KEY THEME

Hampden's case. There has been some debate among historians as to the importance of Hampden's case. It has been argued that it was the first 'nail in the coffin' of Personal Rule, because it encouraged others to resist royal tax demands. However, receipts for ship money do not drop dramatically until 1638. This may have as much to do with resistance to a regular tax demand as with people drawing conclusions from Hampden's case. However, sheriffs found collecting the tax more difficult and were ordered to explain their failure to collect all the sums demanded, with the Royal Council threatening to imprison them.

of fund raising. But, provided he did not go to war, Charles could survive by using these methods. Portland, Treasurer until 1636, increased Crown revenue by some 25 per cent and made some reduction in the royal debt. So, although in debt to the tune of £1,000,000, Charles did, in theory, have the finances to continue with Personal Rule, but however much he squeezed out of 'the system' he could not afford to go to war, so his freedom of action was limited. He needed parliamentary subsidies if he were to have an active foreign policy, or he needed loans from the City of London. Royal financial policies had alienated the City in the 1620s and 1630s. The only group who could be said to be Crown supporters were the customs farmers. When the Scottish crisis came Charles did not have any financial room to manoeuvre, because no one would lend him any money.

The conclusion could be that, compared with some continental monarchs, Charles was solvent, but only in a limited sense. Personal Rule can be seen as a period of 'financial standstill'. A strong, financially independent monarchy was not created in the 1630s. Charles could only 'balance the books' by not going to war, which he could not afford.

LIFE AT COURT UNDER CHARLES I

Charles I's character has already been discussed. His character influenced his tastes and these had a bearing on the life of the court. In the 1630s the court became increasingly alien from the mainstream of English life and a gulf opened between the 'political nation' and the court. The country gentry became suspicious of the court, seeing it as a centre of Roman Catholicism, absolutists and conspiracy.

Charles and Henrietta Maria. Charles was, as has been mentioned, a very private man and a poor communicator. He preferred to surround himself with a small circle of advisers and courtiers – unlike James' court, which, whatever its moral tone, was an 'open one'. After the death of Buckingham, the 'tone' of the court became far more moral, possibly reflecting Charles' new-found affection for Henrietta Maria. They became a devoted couple, and differed on only one issue – religion. She continued not only to be a convinced Catholic herself, but to try to persuade members of the court to convert. Charles had already, in 1627, sent scores of her Catholic attendants back to France but he was unable to persuade her of the virtues of the Church of England, which of course she regarded as a heretic church.

Henrietta Maria's influence. It is probable that, after Buckingham's death, she was a considerable influence on Charles. Judging from her letters to him, as civil war approached, she was quite capable of speaking her mind, although to conclude that Charles was consistently under her influence would be unfair. For instance, she detested both Laud and Strafford, yet Charles trusted them. However, he appears to have done little to prevent the appearance, in the 1630s, of a 'Catholic convert' ring of **Catholics at court** around the queen. Naturally, these Catholic converts, such as Portland and Windibank, were regarded by the country gentry with the greatest suspicion. James' court had been seen by the country gentry as corrupt and immoral, but James did go on hunting trips round the country and was seen by his subjects. Charles' court was 'cleaned up' after Buckingham's death but became a closed inner circle. Charles did not visit the country houses of the gentry and aristocracy as James had done, and the gentry did not come to court.

The culture of the court. The culture of the court set it apart from the country at large. Charles' favoured court architect was Inigo Jones, whose 'neo-classical' style was revolutionary in English terms, but Italian in inspiration. It was Jones who put a new classical front on St Paul's cathedral, and built the queen's Roman Catholic chapel, the Banqueting Hall in Whitehall and the queen's house at Greenwich. They are masterpieces, but Jones' vision reflected the remoteness, and indeed foreignness, of Charles' idea of monarchy. The Banqueting Hall would have reminded people of a European style associated with continental absolutist monarchs. The ceiling painted by Rubens in 1635 has a rather worried-looking James I ascending to heaven. It portrays the divine nature of monarchy as Charles saw it. One of the last sights Charles

KEY THEMES

Catholics at court. Henrietta Maria had her own private chapel and some courtiers, such as Portland and Windibank, changed their religion: they 'converted' from being Protestant to being Catholic, perhaps partly in order to gain influence with her. Her chapel became the centre of a group of court Catholics, and this circle grew.

Henrietta Maria's political views. She saw kingship in continental absolutist terms, not understanding concepts such as common law or Parliament, or indeed anything that could be seen as limiting the king's power.

'The Ascension' by Rubens, from the ceiling of the Banqueting Hall.

saw on earth was the ceiling of the Banqueting Hall before he walked on to the scaffold in 1649.

Court entertainment. Masques were yet another aspect of the 'closed' nature of the court in the 1630s. Ben Jonson, a playwright of genius, collaborated with Inigo Jones, who designed the elaborate costumes – which were used for one performance only. As on the Banqueting Hall ceiling, in their plays – which took the form of **masques** – they held up a mirror to the king, showing what monarchs were supposed to represent to their subjects, and their responsibilities to them. Later masques, written by Jones alone, became totally divorced from reality, showing kingship as divine. The masque was wasteful and extravagant because it lasted for one performance only. However, it was symbolic of the increasing 'dream world' in which the court lived. While Charles was being humiliated by his Scottish subjects in an unsuccessful war, masques portrayed him as a victor.

KEY THEME

The masque. The masque was an art form peculiar to court life. They were plays designed purely for an 'in group' at court who would understand the contents of the plays.

The court and Catholicism. The court in the 1630s bore little resemblance to the lives, prejudices and beliefs of the majority of Charles' subjects. It was seen by many as being not only extravagant, but also papist. The following events strengthened this view.

- The death of **Gustavus Adolphus**. Charles refused to allow the court to go into mourning for the death of King Gustavus II Adolphus in 1632. This was despite the fact that it was the normal protocol (way to behave) for courts to go into mourning for the death of any European monarch, friend or enemy. Charles' refusal only served to confirm the 'country' view of a papist pro-Spanish court.
- Two papal ambassadors (nuncios) attended the court in the late 1630s. No papal representatives had been in England since the break from Rome in 1529.

The court became isolated and dangerously out of touch with the nation – a closed circle whose tastes and attitudes were alien to outsiders. Significantly, in 1632 Charles ordered the gentry to leave the court and live on their estates. By 1639 they had no first-hand knowledge of the court; there was no one to check the rumours of popery and foreign influence.

Masque costume.

KEY THEME

Charles as an art lover. Charles had a reputation as a shrewd collector of art, as shown in his purchase of the Duke of Mantua's collection. It cost him the huge sum, for then, of £18,000. Rubens was paid £3,000 for his portraits of the royal circle.

FOREIGN POLICY

The Thirty Years' War

The views of Charles and Parliament. In 1630–1 Charles made peace with France and Spain. Given his desire not to call a parliament, Charles' foreign-policy options were limited. Even if he had wished to, he could not afford to interfere actively in the Thirty Years' War.

- **Parliament's view.** Despite the failure of Parliament in the 1620s to provide funds for a land-based campaign in Europe in support of the Protestant cause, the country gentry still saw the war in Europe as being a struggle between the forces of true religion – the Dutch Republic, Sweden and the Protestant German states – and the forces of the 'anti-Christ' – the Hapsburgs and the Spanish.

KEY PERSON

Gustavus II Adolphus was King of Sweden from 1594 to 1632. As a Protestant king he involved Sweden in the Thirty Years' War in 1630 with the intention of crushing the Catholic Hapsburg grip on parts of Germany. He was killed at the Battle of Lützen in November 1632.

KEY THEME

Charles' support for Spain. Charles' support for Spain was clear. He not only used the ship-money fleet to protect the Spanish convoys of treasure and troops as they passed up the Channel, he also allowed Spanish troops to be landed, provisioned and rested in England in 1637. His hope was probably that, in exchange for this, his sister Elizabeth, who had married Frederick V of the Palatinate, might be restored with her husband to her rightful inheritance, as Charles had been hoping since the early 1620s. Of course, the Spanish paid well for the concessions they received from Charles.

- **Charles' view.** Charles simply did not share this view. He admired the absolutist states of Spain and Austria and disliked the 'rebellious' Dutch Republic. For Charles there was no great cause in Europe: the Swedish king, for example, was merely interfering in, and prolonging, a war that Charles had no interest in. Despite Henrietta Maria's desire for a pro-French policy, in general Charles pursued a pro-Spanish policy.

As far as the 'country' was concerned, England should have been supporting the Dutch co-religionists, not stabbing them in the back; the pro-Spanish 'neutrality' policy was not popular. Foreign policy was to be a major issue for those who opposed the court in the 1640s. In the late 1630s, the unpopularity of ship money and resistance to its payment were connected with the use that Charles actually made of the fleet that his subjects were reluctantly paying for.

Factors which restricted Charles' choice. With no army, and no means of paying for one, Charles had few foreign-policy options in the 1630s. Some observations can be made on the policy he chose:

- In view of the devastation of continental Europe, his decision to stay out of the 30-year war can be seen as perfectly natural. Foreign observers remarked on the peace and tranquillity England enjoyed in this period.
- Charles' experience with parliaments in the 1620s was such that he could have been justifiably wary about committing England to war for the Protestant cause.
- His important misjudgement was to pursue a 'neutrality' that was not even-handed and was to be remembered in 1640–2 as part of a pro-Catholic conspiracy.

CASE STUDY: NORFOLK DURING PERSONAL RULE

Introduction. Concentration on parliaments and national issues in the seventeenth century does not give a full picture of politics and religion in England as a whole. To most English people what was happening in their locality was more important than events in London. When seventeenth-century people spoke of their 'country', they meant their county. County politics and local issues were the immediate ones. With no parliament sitting, it is hard to judge how Charles' policies were received in the country at large. It is only by looking at England, county by county, that we can get a full picture – for the different counties did not always react uniformly to national issues. For instance, Lancashire, with a large group of Roman Catholics, would present a different picture from, say, Northamptonshire, which had a strong puritan element among the gentry. Norfolk cannot be seen as a 'typical' county, because there was no such thing, but by looking at one county we can at least get some idea of the attitudes of the country at large to Charles' policies.

The Norfolk gentry. The leading gentry families of Norfolk were divided in religion.

- There were Roman Catholic families such as the Bedingfields of Oxburgh and the Cobbs of Sandringham. In general, the Roman Catholic gentry took little part in county affairs, preferring to keep a 'low profile'.
- Examples of 'middle of the road' Church of England families were the L'Estranges of Hunstanton and the Knyvetts of Ashwellthorpe. These gentry were more inclined to support more royal policies than the puritan group.
- A strong puritan element included the Hobarts of Blickling, the Windhams of Felbrigg, the Potts of Mannington and Sir John Holland of Quidenham who, unusually, had a Catholic wife. The puritan element was stronger among the social groups just below the gentry – the yeoman farmers and the prosperous merchants and tradesmen.

There was no one leading gentry family who could be said to control Norfolk politics, as there was in some other counties.

The religious view of the rest of society. Further down the social scale there seems to have been widespread opposition to Laudian ideas. An example of such opposition was that experienced by **Bishop Wren of Norwich**. Some ministers

KEY PEOPLE

The Knyvetts. Moderate Anglicans such as Thomas Knyvett seem to have had little time for Laudian changes, disliking them as much as did the more puritan-minded gentry. When Laud finally ended up in the Tower of London, Knyvett, who was to support the king in the Civil War, could write rather heartlessly to his wife that '[the Archbishop of] Canterbury is still a fattening'. So it appears that someone whose loyalty, in the last resort, was to the Crown, did not like Laud's changes to the way the Church of England conducted its services.

Bishop Wren of Norwich. Wren was bishop between 1635 and 1638. He was a strong Laudian who met a lot of resistance to Laud's instructions from both clergymen and ordinary people. Wren deprived (sacked) at least ten ministers for refusing to obey Laud's instructions and many more had to be pressurised into agreeing with them.

A seventeenth-century map of Norfolk.

and ordinary people 'voted with their feet' and moved to Holland to avoid what they saw as persecution. In all 1,350 people went to Holland between 1636 and 1638. Around 200 people from Norfolk did what Oliver Cromwell had considered doing and went to the 'howling wilderness' of America, leaving Great Yarmouth in April 1637. One of them was a master weaver, Samuel Lewis, whose apprentice went with him. His name was Samuel Lincoln, whose direct descendant was Abraham Lincoln. In general it seems that most people in Norfolk disapproved of Laud's policies, but that may be because more puritan attitudes were widespread in East Anglia.

The 'perfect militia'. In 1628 Charles tried to make the military 'system' in England more effective. He ordered that the militia should be modernised, with more frequent training and new weapons. There was no proper professional army in England and, in theory, all 'able bodied' men could be called up to defend their country. In practice, volunteer

Bishop Wren of Norwich.

companies called 'trained bands' were formed. They occasionally held military gatherings (musters) under officers who were also amateur volunteers from the gentry.

Reluctance in the counties. In most counties, the local gentry and the county as a whole were reluctant to pay for a 'perfect militia', and even more reluctant to pay for the one professional soldier who was to help train them – the 'muster master'. In Somerset the gentry reported to the Royal Council with the casual attitude that they did not know whether the muster master was 'alive or dead'. The whole idea of the 'perfect militia' was sabotaged at county level by the gentry who, although they liked the status of being militia company commanders, were reluctant to force the counties to pay for new equipment and training.

Norfolk's attitude to perfect militias. In Norfolk the gentry came up with rather new ideas to obstruct Charles' plans. They suggested that all the cost of new weapons was unnecessary, proposing that the whole male population of Norfolk could simply turn up on the coast if there was an invasion, armed with clubs with which they could beat invaders to death. Secondly, some of the gentry refused to accept their responsibilities for raising taxes and officering the militia, at least one sending the Lord Lieutenant sick notes from his doctor saying he was unable to ride his horse.

Ship money in Norfolk. In 1636 and 1637 the **collection of ship money** in Norfolk seems to have proceeded without too much difficulty. The amount to be raised for 1637 by Sir William Paston was £7,800 and there seems to have been some resistance to paying. The next sheriff was Sir Francis Astley, who found himself in difficulties in 1638: there were a lot of 'non-payers'. Sir Francis died during his time as sheriff and was replaced by John Buxton, who was to have even more difficulties. His under-sheriff was not hopeful about collecting the full amount required by the king: 'The King hath had almost £30,000 out of this county . . . which makes every sheriff weary of his place.' Eventually Buxton did collect most of the amount required, but only after he had sent 'non-payers' to London to be punished by the Royal Council.

The sheriffs who followed Buxton found their task even more difficult. By 1640 William Windham could collect only £1,100 out of the required £7,800. He was threatened with imprisonment by the Royal Council but even then finally collected only £1,659. The sheriffs in other counties had the same experience. Counties were already paying high militia taxes for the Scottish war (see pp. 93–5), and the taxpayers simply went 'on strike'; there was nothing the sheriffs could do.

Main impressions. The picture of Personal Rule that emerges from Norfolk is of

KEY TERM

Perfect militia. The 'perfect militia' was one of Charles' pet schemes which carried on into Personal Rule. He hoped that the majority of the male population would be trained as amateur soldiers and re-equipped at the cost of each county.

Most importantly, the failure of the scheme at county level showed the limits of Personal Rule. When faced with obstruction by the gentry, who were the only means of carrying out instructions in the counties, the king was powerless.

KEY THEME

Collection of ship money. Ship money was collected by the sheriffs. Being a sheriff marked a gentleman out as a leading figure in the county, but as the 1630s wore on it became a less attractive office than it had been. Sheriffs served for one year.

- a county that, very reluctantly and under pressure, co-operated with the king's policies until 1639, when this co-operation was withdrawn
- a county where Laud's religious policies were deeply unpopular.

A typical puritan country gentleman – Sir Thomas Wodehouse. Attitudes to the court, to Charles' policies and to Archbishop Laud can be illustrated by looking at a 'moderate' Puritan who was perfectly happy in the Church of England until the mid-1630s. Sir Thomas Wodehouse of Kimberley was one of the most influential of the gentry in his county. He came from an 'ancient' family who had been prominent in Norfolk county life for 200 years. Born in 1585, he was a friend and admirer of Henry Prince of Wales, the popular first son of James I. Sir Thomas spent some time at court with Henry. After Henry's death in 1612, Sir Thomas seems to have lost interest in court life, returning to his family home in Norfolk. His interests there were hunting, hawking, books and music. Therefore he did not match the image of a Puritan that some would see as typical. Actually, most puritan gentlemen, except the most extreme, shared Sir Thomas' interests. He took a full part in running his county as the captain of a militia company and a Justice of the Peace. Wodehouse was a moderate, but in 1640 he was to oppose the policies of Charles and Laud, which he saw as extremist and far removed from the moderate tolerant policies of James.

KEY THEME

Wodehouse's poetry. One poem he wrote as a private poem to a friend of his in Suffolk showed his attitudes to what was happening in the 1630s. He wrote of James as 'a good shepard' and regretted his death: 'woe is me now lies he wrapped in lead'. He seems to be less sure of Charles, and especially critical of the Laudian High Church, referring to 'loud organ Laud'. The poem also attacks the policy of giving more power to the Church courts: 'they erect Courts of Commission High'. He seems to have been worried about absolutist tendencies and that Charles had not called a parliament: 'good night to Parliament Petitions of Right'. Ship money is attacked, 'clipping poor sheeps fleeces to pay royal shipping'.

THE DOWNFALL OF PERSONAL RULE

It is important to realise that both the end of Personal Rule and the outbreak of the Civil War were caused by crises not in England but in Charles' other two dominions, **Scotland** and Ireland.

The Scottish crisis

It is an open question whether Charles could have continued to rule without Parliament had he not been overcome by the Scottish crisis, a crisis of his own making. What is certain is that events in Scotland shaped events in England between 1637 and 1640.

Charles had already aroused deep resentment and suspicion among the Scottish nobles, and as time went on things went from bad to worse.

Land. In 1625 Charles had issued an Act of Revocation cancelling all grants of royal land, and of Church land made since 1540. This affected many Scottish landowners, who were unsure whether they would be allowed to keep land that they thought was legally theirs. Church land was an issue that spilt over into religion. Not only did the landowners see themselves as rightful owners of land that had belonged to a Church that had been swept away, but they feared that if Church land returned to the Church it could be the first step to creating a rich, strong Church again, on the Roman Catholic model.

The Act of Revocation also sent shivers down the spines of English gentry who had acquired Church lands in the past one hundred years. They were worried that Charles might find some legal device to do the same thing in England. Certainly Laud would have welcomed such a move.

Laudianism and the new Prayer Book. Charles' coronation in Edinburgh in 1633 was conducted with high-church Laudian ceremonial. This offended the views of the Scots. Laud was determined to bring the Scottish Church into line with what was happening to the English Church. In 1636 he used a royal proclamation to issue new canons (instructions) on the conduct of services, without reference to the General Assembly of the Scottish Church. In 1637, a version of the new 1633 English Prayer Book was introduced. It proved to be a spark that set Scotland aflame.

The Scottish National Covenant 1638. In February 1638 the Scottish National Covenant was drawn up. It rejected the canons and the Prayer Book and eventually opened the way to thoroughgoing Presbyterianism. However, it was left vague enough for nearly everybody to sign it, as it did not specifically outlaw bishops. To Charles, the Covenant spelt open rebellion. Although Charles seemed to be prepared to negotiate with the Scottish Covenanters, in fact he was 'stringing them along' while he prepared for war.

KEY THEME

Scotland. Charles was, of course, King of Scotland and Scotland was a separate kingdom.

Scotland was more feudal than England, with the great landowners and clan chiefs able to command the obedience of a large part of the population.

Scotland was also a more Protestant country than England, especially in the Lowlands. The Scottish bishops had always kept down ceremonies because of deeply held views. Many Scots were Presbyterians, believing in an extreme form of Protestantism.

The combination of an independent-minded population, an absentee king and Calvinism was to be an explosive one. When Charles decided to enforce Laudianism on the Scottish people, he met fierce resistance.

KEY THEME

The new Prayer Book. Congregations in Scotland rioted at the reading of the new Prayer Book. One bishop felt he had to conduct services with loaded pistols in the pulpit. There was a famous stool-throwing incident in St Giles' cathedral in Edinburgh with a woman shouting 'the mass has come amongst us' as she hurled her stool in disgust. Her attitude summed up majority opinion.

Scotland prepares. The Scots, despite **Hamilton's** negotiations, became more determined. In November 1638 the Scottish National Assembly abolished the High Commission and removed the bishops. They also started to raise an army, well aware that Charles was doing the same. The difference was that the Scottish army had a good percentage of professional Scottish soldiers who had been fighting in the Thirty Years' War.

Weaknesses in the English army. Charles' forces were quite different.

- As early as 1628 Charles had called for 'perfect militias', but as these were to be paid for by local taxes, the actual equipment and training of the militias were of poor quality.
- Most militia men had never fired their weapons. In order to save money, 'dry firing' was all that the local gentry commanders would allow; in other words, they practised the loading and aiming without any gunpowder. The Cambridgeshire militia, for example, had the wrong-calibre musket balls for their weapons and half the pikes were useless as the heads had fallen off the rotten poles.
- Professional soldiers, 'muster masters', were supposed to train the militias, but counties often refused to pay their salaries so they drifted off. The gentry, if they had any interest in the militias, were not prepared to take advice from 'low born' soldiers; they commanded their militia companies largely because of the status it gave them in country society, not because they were interested in creating a well-oiled military machine.
- The rank and file were usually poor soldiers, disliked marching out of their own districts, and deserted in large numbers. Many had sympathy for the Scots, who were seen as fellow sufferers. Few wanted to fight for the hated Laudian Prayer Book.

The First Bishops' War 1639. In 1639 Charles spent £185,000 on military operations, while his commander, the Earl of Arundel, found himself unable to launch a successful offensive. Arundel did not improve matters by riding to meet his troops in a coach lent by the papal nuncio, with the papal coat of arms on the doors. This

KEY PERSON

James, First Duke of Hamilton, 1606–49 was a great Scottish landowner. He was Charles' commissioner in Scotland and negotiated with the Scottish Covenanters, but he was not really trusted by either side. Later he was imprisoned by Charles during the First Civil War, but he led Scottish 'Royalist' troops in the Second Civil War (1648). In the end he was executed by Parliament.

KEY ISSUE

Military failure. The poor discipline and incompetence of the majority of the militias is not a minor point.

- Firstly, given Charles' grand plans for perfect militias, they show the gap between the appearance and the reality of Personal Rule. Without the wholehearted co-operation of the local gentry, Charles could not create a viable military force – surely one of the most important elements in a powerful independent monarchy.
- Secondly, had the militias been efficient, Charles might have won the Bishops' Wars, or at least not suffered the humiliating defeats that led directly to the crisis of 1640.

only confirmed the idea that this was a papist war against honest Protestants. Once again Charles, his advisers and ministers misunderstood 'public opinion'. To try to improve matters, the Earl of Strafford was recalled from Ireland, but he could not retrieve the situation. In these circumstances Strafford, perhaps out of touch with English affairs after having been so long in Ireland, advised the king to call a parliament, expecting, in this crisis, that traditional loyalty to the Crown would reassert itself and a parliament would vote money for an offensive to crush the Scottish rebellion. The City of London had a poor relationship with Charles and was not prepared to lend him money.

Charles had few options.

- His military costs were estimated at £600,000 for 1640 and his high-handed treatment of the City of London came home to roost when a request for a loan of £100,000 was rejected and a £10,000 gift offered instead.
- When he did call Parliament it was not because he had suddenly been converted to the idea of partnership

Thomas Howard, second Earl of Arundel.

between Crown and Parliament. Neither had he come to see Personal Rule as a mistake. He called Parliament because he had no choice. Only Parliament could provide the funds for a war to reassert royal authority in Scotland.

THE SHORT PARLIAMENT, APRIL–MAY 1640

The Short Parliament proved to be a great disappointment to Charles. From the beginning, distrust of Charles was evident. MPs were reluctant to support a war against fellow Protestants who had rebelled against Laudianism. It should be noted that the comments of MPs were not directed at Charles himself but at Laud and his other advisers, and the Roman Catholic circle at court. While these people had influence over Charles, Parliament was not going to grant the twelve subsidies that Charles requested, even though he linked these to an abandonment of ship money.

The settling of 'grievances'. The Commons, led by Pym, demanded that 'grievances' be dealt with before subsidies could be voted. At this point Laud, characteristically, inflamed the situation by issuing a new set of **canons** (instructions) with clear support for divine right.

The king, rather than haggle with Parliament, which he regarded as beneath his dignity, dissolved Parliament after only three weeks in May 1640. It was to prove a serious mistake, as attitudes were to harden after the dissolution. At least in the Short Parliament there had been a significant minority who were supportive of Charles.

The Second Bishops' War 1640. In July, Charles had confiscated bullion (gold and silver coinage) held in the Tower of London for safe keeping by English merchants. After toying with a scheme to use it as a basis for new coins mixed with copper (thus creating a less pure, 'debased', coinage with a smaller amount of gold or silver in it), Charles held on to £30,000 worth as a 'loan'. This, of course, did nothing for his already strained relations with the City of London merchants. These were desperate measures which could not save the situation.

KEY THEMES

MPs' attitude towards Scotland in 1640. The rejection of the new Prayer Book changed many MPs' attitudes towards the Scots. Instead of being viewed as cronies at James I's court, looking to England as a land of milk and honey, the Scots now became heroic Protestant rebels.

Laud's canons 1640. Every church minister was to read aloud the following: 'The most high and sacred order of Kings is of divine nature … a supreme power is given to this most excellent order by God himself … Kings should rule and command all persons of rank or estate soever . . .'.

KEY THEMES

Strafford's advice in May 1640. Strafford had urged the calling of a parliament in 1640 but now took a hard line. He advised Charles, 'goe on with a vigorous war, as you first designed, loose and absolved from all rules of government . . . they refusing you are acquitted towards God and man, you have an army in Ireland, you may employ it here to reduce this Kingdome'. This advice was to prove fatal for Strafford later on.

Strafford's description. 'the army altogether necessitate and unprovided . . . that part which I bring now from Durham, the worst [I] ever saw. Our horse [cavalry] all cowardly; the country from Berwick to York in the power of the Scots, a universal affright [fear] in all, a general disaffection to the King's service, non sensible of his dishonour.'

The failure of the Short Parliament was followed by the outbreak of new fighting with the Scots. At a skirmish at Newcastle upon Tyne in August 1640 the English were beaten. **Strafford's description** of the Scottish advance in August helps to explain why the Scots were able to capture Newcastle, cutting off London's vital coal supply, and occupy the six northern counties.

The war was ended by the the Treaty of Ripon of October 1640. Negotiated by the Council of Peers, it was a complete humiliation for Charles. The Scots secured £850 to cover the costs of their occupation of Northumberland and Durham, but also, in effect, as their price for not moving further south. In these circumstances, defeated, and unable to pay the costs of the Scottish occupation, Charles had no choice but to call another parliament to vote the subsidies required. Personal Rule had finally collapsed and Parliament was called for 3 November 1640.

SUMMARY QUESTIONS

1 Why did Archbishop Laud arouse so much suspicion and dislike?

2 What were the main financial policies of Personal Rule, and why was there so much opposition to them?

3 Why did the Scots rebel and what was the result of the Scottish Wars?

4 Why, by 1640, was there a widespread belief in a Roman Catholic 'absolutist' conspiracy to undermine the ancient ways and constitution as well as the Church of England?

5 Why did Personal Rule collapse?

CHAPTER 5

From crisis to civil war 1640–2

THE ELECTION OF THE LONG PARLIAMENT

The formation of the 'anti-court consensus'. The elections to the Long Parliament probably saw more people voting than at any time before the nineteenth century. In some cases, sheriffs probably did not even check in county elections that all voters were eligible to vote. As a result, vast crowds voted and the majority of MPs were well aware of the views of their constituents. 'Choose no court papist, ship money sheriff' was the cry and those candidates who had been associated with royal practices in the 1630s went down to crushing defeat.

By November 1640 the country gentry going up to Parliament were united in a set of negative attitudes, with a fairly clear idea of what they wanted to stop.

- They were determined to stop what they saw as the slide of the Church into Catholicism. They believed that Laudian changes had to be reversed.
- They wanted to punish or neutralise the king's 'evil advisers', namely Windibank, Finch and especially Laud and Strafford.
- They also wanted to restore the old constitutional balance between the rights of the subject and the rights of the king, believing that the last ten years had seen an attempt to set up a semi-absolutist state on the continental model.
- They wished to eliminate the financial innovations of Personal Rule, such as forest fines and ship money.
- They wished to get rid of the hated Court of Wards, which had doubled its income during Personal Rule.
- The Prerogative Courts, Star Chamber and High Commission were also marked down for elimination.

KEY THEME

'Anti-court consensus'. When historians use this modern term they are referring to the majority of MPs who assembled in November 1640. These MPs agreed that the court's policies had to be stopped. A consensus is a general agreement or a shared attitude.

The belief in an absolutist Roman Catholic conspiracy. More generally and most importantly, there was a widespread belief in a Roman Catholic conspiracy, which was centred on members of the court and which was working away to undermine the 'ancient constitution'. Therefore Parliament wished to 'free' the king from these evil influences.

KEY THEME

The attitude of MPs. It is most important that we do not expect the MPs to have had the same motives in 1640 as they had by 1642 or 1648. Had the conservative country gentry of 1640 realised what was to happen by 1642, and by 1649, they would have acted very differently. We know the end of the story, they did not.

The attitude of MPs. Looking at the situation objectively, the king was in a weak position in November 1640, but the country gentry coming up to Parliament did not come up feeling confident that they had the upper hand. There was a general feeling that this might be the last chance to reverse the trends of the 1630s before England became a Roman Catholic-dominated, absolutist state. Apprehension went hand in hand with confidence that the country supported them. Much of that apprehension centred on the person of Strafford, whose record in Ireland and in the Council of the North indicated a minister who could ruthlessly get things done, and could make absolutism work.

So the anti-court consensus, with its fear of a Roman Catholic conspiracy and its hatred of the court and the king's ministers, was united in what it wanted to prevent, what it wanted to destroy, but the majority had no forward-looking programme of reform, no real idea of creating a new constitution giving more power to the Commons and taking power from the Crown.

The aim of MPs in 1640. They had come up to London to 'restore' the old constitution as they saw it. It was not their aim to start a revolution. In that sense they can be seen as 'conservative', and the fact that, with the exception of the 60 or so 'court MPs' who supported the Crown, they were united on what they disliked, does not mean that they shared a vision of what the future should hold. The cement that held them together was negative: fear of popery, fear of absolutism. Nobody in 1640 could have known what was to happen by 1642 – that a section of Parliament would find itself at war with the king – and nobody could possibly have even contemplated armed rebellion against the king, let alone his eventual execution in 1649.

THE FIRST SESSION OF THE LONG PARLIAMENT 1640–1

The new parliament first met on 3 November 1640. The first targets of the 'anti-court consensus' were the king's 'evil advisers'. These included **Finch** and **Windibank**, who fled abroad. Archbishop Laud was arrested and sent to the Tower, eventually to be executed in 1645. The main target, however, was Strafford.

The fall of Strafford. Strafford's record in government made him the most marked man in England. He and Laud had been most associated with the policy of **thorough**. In 1628 he 'changed sides', but from his point of view parliaments had only a limited role: they were there to support the Crown. After the Petition of Right of 1628

KEY PEOPLE

Finch and **Windibank** were two of the main agents of Personal Rule. They were Roman Catholic converts associated with Henrietta Maria and particularly distrusted and hated by the House of Commons.

KEY TERM

Thorough. The policy of 'thorough' was the ruthless carrying out of royal wishes, and extension of royal authority without regard for individuals or the law.

Thomas Wentworth, Earl of Strafford.

Strafford believed the king should have expected support from Parliament. Therefore it was logical to further his own career and support royal policies. He had also managed to make a lot of money, but no more than any other seventeenth-century statesman.

Strafford in Ireland. In 1633 Strafford went to Ireland as Lord Deputy. He reduced Ireland to obedience, something never before achieved, but as a result he came to be hated in Ireland and feared in England, for the English gentry took the view that what he had done in Ireland he could do in England. The Irish Parliament was reduced to a 'rubber stamp', just voting taxes to support Strafford's new Irish army. The Protestant Church of Ireland was remodelled on Laudian lines, much to the resentment of the Scottish Presbyterian settlers of Ulster. Strafford also made sure that powerful individuals knew their place. The most notable of these was the Earl of Cork, who alleged that Strafford had taken £40,000 of his personal estate and ignored the law in doing so.

Strafford is impeached. The Commons were determined to eliminate the threat of such a ruthless and dynamic minister. On 11 November 1640, Strafford was impeached by Parliament. The main charge was that he wished to bring his Irish army over to use as a force to continue Personal Rule by setting up a royal military dictatorship. The advice that he had given to Charles after the dissolution of the Short Parliament now rebounded on him.

Strafford's execution 1641. Evidence of actual treachery was difficult to obtain, so Pym had to resort to an **act of attainder**, which needed less precise evidence. The **London mob** were putting pressure on the Lords to pass the act. Many in the House of Lords were becoming worried about the implications of such a vague legal charge. However, they passed the act under the impression that Charles would never sign it. He had already promised Strafford that he would not suffer in 'either life or fortune' but, as so often under pressure, Charles wavered and Strafford was executed on 12 May on Tower Hill in front of a crowd of around 100,000 people. It appears that Charles was really worried about a popular uprising if he did not pass the act,

KEY THEMES

Ireland had always been a thorn in the side of royal administrators. The great Anglo-Irish lords and landowners and the Scottish Presbyterian settlers were independent of London and used to being able to do as they wished. The Roman Catholic Irish, who were gradually being pushed out of their lands by the Scots and English, resented English government from a different point of view.

An act of attainder was an act of Parliament which stated that the accused person was guilty of treason. Its appeal for Pym and others was that less evidence had to be provided. The act was simply passed by Parliament in the usual way.

KEY TERM

The London mob was mainly made up of apprentice boys. They were strongly Protestant in their views.

A contemporary engraving showing the trial of the Earl of Strafford.

but Laud's comment is pointed: 'he [Strafford] served a mild and gracious prince who knew not how to be, nor could be made great'.

The destruction of the machinery of Personal Rule. The House of Commons, with Pym orchestrating, assaulted all the machinery of Personal Rule. Star Chamber and High Commission were abolished, which deprived the king and the Church of their most powerful legal weapons. On top of that, acts were passed with the following effects.

- Ship money was declared illegal.
- The boundaries of royal forests were declared to be those of the twentieth year of James' reign.
- Distraint of knighthood was declared illegal.
- The Court of Wards was abolished.

The Triennial Act 1641. All these acts, to which Charles assented, however reluctantly, can be seen as re-establishing the 'old constitution'. One act, signed by Charles on the same day that he signed Strafford's attainder, was new. The Triennial Act of May 1641 laid down that a parliament must be called every three years and thus took away the royal prerogative of calling parliaments. This was followed by an act which laid down that the present parliament could be dismissed only by its own consent. In other words, Charles could no longer get rid of Parliament as he wished.

Why did Charles agree? These measures were 'revolutionary', and why Charles agreed to them is, on the face of it, puzzling.

- It is possible that as he was agonising over Strafford's fate he failed to realise the full significance of what he was agreeing to.
- The London mob, probably encouraged by Pym's supporters in the City, was active.
- Charles may well have seen these as temporary concessions. When in the future he was in a stronger position, he would be able to withdraw again.

Pym's control of the House of Commons. Until the summer of 1641 the anti-court consensus held reasonably intact, although some members already had misgivings about the legality of Strafford's execution and about an 'act for a perpetual Parliament'. That the 'consensus' held is partly due to Pym's skill. He and his associates, such as **Sir Henry Vane** and **Oliver St John**, were able to present these measures as being necessary to safeguard the freedoms of the House of Commons and as restoring the balance of the constitution. Pym was particularly good at playing on fears of popery, and he fully supported the idea that there was a Roman Catholic conspiracy that still needed to be fully dealt with. A vague 'army plot' in the spring of 1641, involving officers around the court possibly planning a *coup d'état*, only helped Pym's thesis.

The events of 1641–2 can only be fully understood in the light of the great fear of such a conspiracy, and the atmosphere of crisis in which the Long Parliament was meeting, at least for some of the time.

KEY PEOPLE

Sir Henry Vane was a leading puritan politician. He played an important role in the impeachment of Strafford. From 1642 he was a leading member of the war party and he was a leader of the House of Commons after Pym's death in 1643. He later became a republican.

Oliver St John was a leading figure in the Hampden case over ship money, when he had defended Hampden. He was a fierce critic of Strafford and later became a republican.

Maſter PYM
HIS SPEECH
In Parliament, on Wedneſday, the
fifth of January, 1641,
Concerning the Vote of the Houſe of Commons,
for his diſcharge upon the Accuſation of High
Treaſon, exhibited againſt himſelfe, and the
Lord Kimbolton, Mr. John Hampden, Sr.
Arthur Haſterig, Mr. Strowd,
M. Hollis, by his Maieſty.

The true Effigies of Mr. John Pym, Eſquire

London Printed for I. W, 1641.

An engraving of the front of a printed speech by John Pym in 1641.

The death of Bedford, May 1641. A significant event in May 1641 was the death of Francis Russell, Earl of Bedford. Bedford was a 'man with a foot in both camps'; he was a courtier but had good relations with some of the leading men in Parliament. Pym had a seat over which Bedford had control and Pym also looked after some of the Russell family affairs. Bedford was a 'moderate' and probably hoped to organise a government that would have the confidence of the House of Commons, the Lords and the king. A bridge between Parliament and the king could possibly have been constructed by Bedford. St John had become Solicitor General in January 1641 (he was a close associate of Pym), and several 'opposition peers', including Bedford and Essex, had been appointed to the Royal

KEY EVENT

The significance of the death of Bedford. If anyone could have built a 'government of national confidence', it was Bedford, for he had access to, and was listened to by, Charles. His death removed a very important chance of compromise.

Council. By May 1641 it seemed that Bedford was arranging for Pym to be Chancellor of the Exchequer, while the Secretary of State was to be Denzil Holles, at that time a Pym associate.

The Ten Propositions 1641. By the summer Pym had set out his position in the Ten Propositions, which included a request to the king that he commit 'his own business and the affairs of the Kingdom to such councillors and officers as the Parliament may have cause to confide in'. This demand, that Parliament should in effect choose the king's ministers, would, like the Triennial Act, take away some of the king's prerogative powers, but from that moment on Pym never wavered in this aim. Given that the demand was 'revolutionary', why did a 'conservative' House of Commons accept it? There are several explanations.

- Pym presented his demands as being 'defensive', ensuring that all the laws passed already would be protected through some control over ministers who had access to the king.
- Until the Grand Remonstrance of November 1641, or indeed the Nineteen Propositions of June 1642, many members may not have understood the significance of Pym's position.
- After the collapse of the hopes that many had held of Bedford, not because of Charles' opposition but because of Bedford's death, it may have seemed a reasonable demand which the king would have been inclined to accept.
- The problem was 'glossed over' by the king's decision to go north and visit Scotland, and a six-week recess of Parliament.

The Root and Branch Petition. One potentially divisive issue had already been raised in February 1641. The London Root and Branch Petition called for the abolition of bishops. Many MPs had no love for high-handed Laudian bishops but that did not mean they wished to see bishops abolished altogether. Most wanted the moderate bishops of Elizabeth's time, not a **Presbyterian system**. Pym, whatever his private views, realised this issue was one which could divide the Commons, so he deflected it in the

KEY TERM

A **Presbyterian system** was a Church without bishops. This worried many in England, who feared that removing bishops would be a first step to changing the social and political structure.

usual style of a politician with an awkward problem: it was given to a committee to discuss – the Assembly of Divines.

Conclusion to the first session of the Long Parliament.

- The majority of the country MPs were satisfied with the first session of the Long Parliament. There was still a lurking fear of a Roman Catholic conspiracy, and some MPs were beginning to have doubts about Pym's use of the mob to pressurise the Lords into passing measures. However, Pym's skill at keeping the Commons together meant that, until the summer of 1641, the Commons were reasonably united.
- Despite the general unanimity of the first session, under the surface there were cracks that Pym was plastering over. Important questions remained about the question of the future organisation of the Church and the role of Parliament in relation to the Crown. Most MPs wished to maintain a balanced constitution.
- More broadly, the aims of the anti-court consensus had largely been achieved by the summer of 1641, so where was Parliament to go next? Was there any need for further legislation? Could Charles now be trusted to rule in a 'mixed constitution' and not return to his absolutist leanings if Parliament dissolved itself? In the summer of 1641 these questions were mostly unspoken, but they were there in the minds of many MPs.

Pym's achievement had been to keep the mainly negative anti-court consensus together, but this was going to become increasingly difficult. However, distrust of Charles was still a strong factor holding Parliament together.

Charles in Scotland. In August 1641 Charles left for Scotland to ratify the **treaty** between the two countries. In England there was a fear that he hoped to woo the Scots into providing him with an army. Parliament actually sent commissioners with him with a 'watching brief'. Events in Scotland only fuelled doubts about Charles' trustworthiness. Although some Scots were by now disillusioned with the Covenanters, most were very wary of Charles. This followed an incident in October 1641 in which extremist Scottish royalists led by the Marquis of Montrose (in prison during the king's visit to Scotland)

KEY EVENT

The treaty with Scotland 1641. The aim of the treaty was to make peace between the two sides. The Scottish and English armies were to be paid off with the proceeds of a poll tax granted by Parliament.

tried to capture the Covenanter leaders, including the Earl of Argyll. The result was that any hope of Charles coming to an agreement with his Scottish subjects was destroyed. Charles may not have known of 'the incident' but in England parallels were drawn with the 'army plot' and Charles' integrity was again damaged.

THE SECOND SESSION OF THE LONG PARLIAMENT 1641–2

When Parliament re-assembled in October 1641 the potential splits began to be apparent. Pym was convinced that Charles was not to be trusted – that, if Parliament did not put further restraints on royal power, once Parliament dissolved itself Charles would go back to his 'absolutist tendencies'.

KEY THEME

Henrietta Maria's political views. The queen hated parliaments. In her view kings ruled and subjects obeyed. She certainly encouraged Charles to resist Parliament's demands. She also encouraged some of the more hot-headed members of her circle into considering military coups to remove the 'rebellious' leaders of the Commons.

The role of Henrietta Maria. Having eliminated the previous 'evil advisers', Pym now saw Henrietta Maria and her associates at court as being the dangerous influence over Charles. Henrietta Maria never understood the ideas behind the English constitution. In such sensitive times her ignorance was to be of critical importance.

KEY PERSON

Sir Edward Hyde, later Earl of Clarendon, was to become one of the most prominent royalists. In 1640 he had supported the opposition to Charles and had joined in the attack on Strafford. However, he disliked the proposal to exclude bishops from the House of Lords and opposed the Grand Remonstrance (see p. 107).

Support for Charles appears. At the same time, a group emerged in the House of Commons who could be called the 'Constitutional Royalists'. Their leading members were **Sir Edward Hyde** and Viscount Falkland. These were true 'conservatives'. They had opposed the royal policies of the 1630s as being radical and undermining the constitution. They had disliked Laudian changes to the Church and had agreed to the execution of Strafford. Now their 'conservatism' made them concerned for the future. To conservatives such as Hyde the reforms of 1641 had restored the balance between the king and Parliament. The Church of England was now back to its proper position with the fall of the Laudian bishops. Their concern was that now extremist Puritans would actually destroy the Church of England and that Pym's policies would lead to constitutional change or, worse, anarchy. They believed that now the king must be trusted or the constitution could not work.

Sir Edward Hyde.

Charles' growing popularity. Had Charles consistently taken the advice of the Constitutional Royalists, it is quite possible that he would have averted disaster. Many MPs were sympathetic to their views and there are signs that in the autumn of 1641 Charles was becoming more popular. This may be partly due to the increasing activities of religious radicals, with growth of unauthorised preaching and disturbances in churches. There was also unrest in many towns and cities, which was partly caused by a trade depression. In these circumstances the king represented stability.

Charles fails to keep to a consistent attitude. If Charles had consistently followed the moderate constitutional path advised by Hyde and Falkland, he could have presented himself as

- the symbol of order and stability,
- a trustworthy monarch who would rule according to the law, respecting his subjects' rights while protecting his own rights.

This might have undermined Pym's position. Pym's use of the London mob and his apparent desire to push on with further constitutional changes were beginning to cause alarm in the House of Commons among the naturally conservative gentry. Pym was determined to press on because he genuinely believed in a Roman Catholic underground conspiracy manipulating the king. He also feared for his own life if the king were to regain total freedom of action. He was aware of the sort of advice Charles was getting from Henrietta Maria and that he was tempted to follow it. The gradual erosion of the anti-court consensus, Pym's fears about Charles' motives and the Roman Catholic circle at court; all these led Pym to what could be seen not as a self-confident sign of a strong position, but as a desperate measure – the **Grand Remonstrance.**

KEY EVENT

The Grand Remonstrance started by listing all the policies and actions of Charles that had caused the Commons to distrust him. It then made some demands which it justified because of the previous track record of Charles and his ministers. The main points included:

- Parliament should choose the king's ministers.
- Parliament should be able to remove the king's ministers.
- There should be a conference of religious ministers to reform the Church of England.
- There was a Roman Catholic conspiracy to undermine the constitution and religion of England; the Commons should investigate it and have the right to punish those involved.

The break-up of the anti-court consensus. The Grand Remonstrance was the rock on which the 'anti-court consensus' finally broke up. It was drawn up during October and presented to the Commons in November 1641. Much of the Remonstrance can be seen as propaganda. It was designed to do the following:

- remind members of the past actions of Charles,
- re-assert the existence of a Roman Catholic conspiracy,
- justify what were clearly 'revolutionary' demands – the right of the Commons to choose the king's ministers (harking back to the Ten Propositions of May) and control of the militia.

These were clear invasions of the royal prerogative and could not be seen as restoring the 'old constitution'. The Remonstrance divided the House of Commons. After heated debates, including drawn swords in the House, it was passed by 159 votes to 148.

Consequences of the Grand Remonstrance. There was now the making of a 'king's party' in the House, prepared to defend the old constitution. Many MPs were concerned about certain aspects of the Remonstrance and how it had been introduced.

- Many members had been disturbed by Pym's use of the mob to put pressure for a favourable vote.
- **The Remonstrance was printed** and published and this, for many conservatives, was the last straw. In other words, the conservative gentry, already very disturbed by Pym's willingness to use the mob to bring political pressure on the House of Lords, were horrified that 'the people' were being involved in politics by Pym's publication of the Remonstrance.
- Pym was seen as undermining social and political order.
- Some MPs were already very disturbed at the signs of public disorder, with authorised preaching, floods of pamphlets and rioting. Anarchy could now be seen as a threat as great as Charles' absolutist policies.

The Irish rebellion – the crisis deepens. However, another event took place which made the crisis worse. On 1 November the news broke of a rebellion in Ireland. Now that the oppressive rule of Strafford had been removed, the Catholic native Irish had risen in rebellion against the Ulster Presbyterians. Probably 4,000 Protestants died in massacres and perhaps another 8,000 from exposure as they were forced to leave their homes in the winter. Horror stories, which lost nothing in the telling, abounded and absurd estimates of the numbers killed circulated. The consequences of the revolt were damaging for Charles.

- The rebels claimed, falsely, to be acting in his name.
- As the full implications of the revolt sank in, one question was paramount. An army would have to be raised to put down the rebellion and the king had the

KEY THEMES

Opposition to the printing of the Grand Remonstrance. Sir Edward Dering, a Kent MP who had supported all the changes of the past year, spoke for many when he said, 'I did not dream that we should remonstrate downwards, tell tales to the people and speak of the King as of a third person.'

The king's reply to the Remonstrance. The king's reply to the Remonstrance was measured. It was designed to reassure members that while he was prepared to defend his legal rights, he was also defending the rights of his subjects. Had he continued to follow the advice of the moderate royalists, it is possible that he would have won over more members of Parliament and that Pym's position would have crumbled.

undoubted right to command the army. But many in England felt that Charles could not be trusted with an army.
- The Irish rebellion also strengthened the belief in a Roman Catholic conspiracy.

Charles' mistakes during the crisis. The Irish rebellion was the turning point of the period from 1640 to 1642. For too long Charles had given the impression that he was still hoping to regain the position he had held in the 1630s.

Another problem was that Charles was inconsistent in following policy. At the end of 1641, feeling more self-confident, he turned to advice from the group at court which surrounded Henrietta Maria. Charles made a mistake in the appointment of **Thomas Lunsford** as Governor of the Tower of London. This was an important appointment because the Governor of the Tower of London could intimidate the City. To many in the capital the appointment of Lunsford seemed to be a confirmation of Charles' secret desire to regain freedom of action through a military coup. However, under pressure Charles cancelled the appointment. He sent two equally damaging signals: firstly, that he had thought about a coup, but secondly, that he was weak and could be forced to back down.

KEY PEOPLE

Thomas Lunsford was a soldier of fortune. His type of person was popularly supposed to be the sort of adventurer who would involve himself in a military coup.

George Digby, second Earl of Bristol, 1612–77. By 1641 he was the principal adviser to Henrietta Maria. He consistently undermined attempts by the Constitutional Royalists to persuade Charles into a moderate line. He was a Roman Catholic convert, a leading figure in the Five Members Coup and continued as a damaging absolutist influence over Charles. He intrigued against other royalist advisers and successful royalist commanders in the Civil War and later fled to France. His advice to Charles was usually disastrous, both before and during the Civil War.

The next mistake Charles made was not to appoint the Earl of Essex as commander of the troops to be raised for the re-conquest of Ireland. That was a military appointment that would have reassured the House of Commons. Essex was associated with all the 'reforms' of the past year. In the end, Charles failed to nominate a commander.

The Five Members Coup, 3 January 1642. Still listening to Digby and Henrietta Maria, Charles then made a fatal error. Believing that an impeachment of the queen was being plotted by Pym and his supporters, he ordered the impeachment of Lord Mandeville, of the House of Lords, and Pym, Hampden, Strode, Haselrige and Holles, the so-called five members (of the House of Commons). The impeachment sent to the Lords was not acted on, and Charles decided on what was, in effect, a military coup. On 5 January 1642 he entered the House of Commons

Charles I entering the House of Commons, with 300 troops, on 5 January 1642.

with 300 troops to arrest the five members. They had been tipped off, escaped and were safely in the City.

The effects of the Five Members Coup

- The Commons were outraged by this breach of privilege. The king was surrounded by an angry mob as he left the Commons and the five members returned in triumph. Given the temper of the population, Charles seems to have literally feared for his life and on 10 January he left London.
- The whole affair of the five members made civil war more likely.
- It swung many MPs back to Pym, as this was what he had been predicting: a military coup encouraged by Roman Catholics.
- The king's departure from London was also crucial. It created a situation of two sides negotiating at a distance.

Charles' inconsistent behaviour. It is difficult to judge what Charles was preparing to do once he had left London. At first he attempted to gain control of arsenals at Portsmouth, Kingston upon Thames and, most importantly, Hull. He failed. The queen left for France to seek support for her husband and then Charles appears to have listened to the advice of Hyde again. Hyde started to produce moderate royalist propaganda that was quite convincing. However, the inconsistent pattern of Charles' behaviour was the same as before. Charles swung between concession and compromise on the one hand and active preparations for war on the other.

KEY THEME

The advice of Henrietta Maria to Charles in 1642. Henrietta Maria's advice to Charles was consistently 'no compromise'. A letter of hers to Charles in March 1642 gives a flavour of her views: 'a report is current here that you are returning to London . . . I believe nothing of it and hope you are more constant in your resolutions, you have already learnt, to your cost, that want of perseverance . . . has ruined you. But if it be so adieu: for assuredly you will never change my resolution to retire into a convent, for I can never trust myself to those persons who would be your directors, nor to you sire, you would have broken your promise to me.'

The drift to civil war, January–July 1642. 'We sink unsensibly into this state of civil war' was the comment of Sir Harbottle Grimston, and in some ways he was right. Developments during the period January to August 1642 made any compromise impossible.

- **Unrest.** There was widespread social disorder, including rioting in the Stour valley among the weavers, and in the Fens. A poor harvest and a trade depression – 'the trade of this Kingdom stoppeth altogether', noted the Venetian ambassador with some exaggeration – meant that there was considerable distress among the lower orders. The gentry found these signs of unrest most disturbing to the social order, and the growth of radical preaching and pamphleteering also seemed to threaten stability.
- **The gentry arms itself.** In these circumstances some of the gentry were arming themselves, fearing the country would slide into anarchy. The reason for this was that, in practice, there had developed two rival authorities – the king in the north and Parliament in London. A potential power vacuum was therefore being created, and the collapse of the authority of the Church of England only made the future seem bleaker for those who saw the cement that held society together beginning to crumble.
- **Propaganda war.** Throughout the spring and summer, a 'paper war' was conducted between the king and Parliament, each hoping to persuade the uncommitted, or moderates, of the justice of their cause and to convince the other side of their strength.

KEY TERM

The Militia Ordinance 1642. This ordinance ordered the appointing of officers to the militia, with orders that they make sure the militia was prepared.

The Militia Ordinance and Commission of Array, March 1642. In March 1642 Parliament took another step on the road to war by issuing the **Militia Ordinance**. In theory, only the king could do this, but naturally he refused parliamentary requests that they should appoint the Deputy Lieutenants and officers. In these circumstances Parliament acted alone to put the country into 'a posture of defence by authority of both houses'. The king replied with a 'call-up' that was legally even more dubious – the **Commission of Array**. Both sides then were trying to secure the county militias to frighten the other into surrender. In fact, the Commission of Array, a very ancient legal device, was not accepted by many.

- The king did not have a great deal of success in getting the county militias to support him. By the summer, Parliament's position seemed to be stronger militarily, despite Hyde's skilful royalist propaganda.
- The majority of the gentry either supported the Militia Ordinance 'for the defence of the King and Parliament', or seemed to be trying to be neutral.

KEY THEME

Rejection of the Commission of Array. A judge in the West Country noted in a letter to the king, 'the truth is the counties are much possessed with the illegality of the Commissions of Array and the unlimited power as is alleged in the Commissions'.

The Nineteen Propositions, June 1642. Pym then felt confident enough to present the Nineteen Propositions to the king. These were Parliament's final approach to the king. However, the demands left little room for compromise. They were:

- that the king give up some of his prerogatives, such as control of the armed forces,
- that Parliament should choose the king's ministers,
- that the King agree to the Militia Ordinance,
- that Parliament should control Church matters,
- that Parliament should appoint guardians for the king's children.

These demands would have made Charles almost a constitutional monarch in the modern sense of the term. As it was, Charles was left with no choice. For a king who believed in divine right, acceptance of the propositions would have been unthinkable.

Charles declares war. As a result of the rejection of the Nineteen Propositions, Parliament appointed a committee of public safety and put the Earl of Essex in charge of 24,000 soldiers.

Charles formally raised his standard at Nottingham on 22 August and declared war on Parliament. Pym probably thought, as did others, that this was an empty, futile gesture. The king had only 800 supporters with him and therefore, if there was to be any fighting, there would be only a skirmish or two before Charles saw the logic of his position and accepted the Nineteen Propositions.

KEY THEME

Concerns about the drift into war. Many of the English gentry would have been mystified as to how England had 'drifted into this state of Civil War', a war that probably nobody, except a few hot-heads mostly on the king's side, wanted. Even at this stage, it is possible that the crisis could have been settled 'with some showers of blood', rather than 'effusions of blood', as Thomas Knyvett hoped.

Parliament miscalculates. The parliamentary leaders had badly miscalculated. The first civil war was to last four years and it cost the lives of at least 50,000 Englishmen. Parliament's next move, again probably the result of over-confidence, ensured that at last the king got a sizeable army. On 6 September a parliamentary declaration stated that those who did not actively support Parliament were to be declared 'delinquents' and pay for the cost of the war.

This finally drove those members of the gentry who wished to remain neutral into making up their minds. Neutrality was no longer an option for them. When pushed into making a choice, their leanings were towards the royalist side and within weeks the king had a sizeable army. A long war had begun.

SUMMARY QUESTIONS

1 What did most MPs want in 1640?

2 Why were the vast majority of MPs determined to execute Strafford and imprison Laud?

3 Why was the death of the Duke of Bedford so important?

4 What was Pym's role in the period 1640–2, and why was he so important?

5 Why did the Irish Rebellion make the crisis so much worse?

6 What mistakes did Charles make between 1640 and 1642?

7 Why, by the spring of 1642, did civil war seem possible?

8 Who was more responsible for the final breakdown into civil war – Charles or Pym?

CHAPTER 6

The Civil Wars and the execution of Charles I 1642–9

STRENGTHS AND WEAKNESSES OF THE TWO SIDES

Parliament's strengths

- Parliament controlled the more populated and prosperous part of the kingdom, as well as that vital source of wealth – London.
- Once Pym had set up efficient tax-gathering mechanisms, Parliament's war finances were on a much sounder footing than were Charles'.
- Parliament's control of the Navy meant a control of trade. Therefore Parliament was able to ensure that London could continue to be England's trading capital. It also restricted Charles' ability to trade with the continent for military supplies.

Charles' strengths and weaknesses

- The king had advantages over Parliament in the early months of the war. His cavalry was probably better and he had a cavalry commander of great talent in his German nephew, **Prince Rupert**.
- Financial problems. The king's area of control was the poorer north and west. Charles had to rely on individual gifts, plus the gold and silver plate given by Oxford colleges, and the fact that many of his commanders paid their troops out of their own pocket. Although Royalist fund-raising in some areas was well organised, in general, as time went on, the king's shortage of money became one of the major factors in his eventual defeat – 'the incurable disease of want of money', as Clarendon described it.
- In theory, the Royalist war effort should have been more co-ordinated as Charles was Commander-in-Chief but, in a mirror of his court in the period before 1642, faction and rivalries undermined the common cause. Digby did his best to turn Charles against his field

KEY PERSON

Prince Rupert was an inspiring leader of cavalry. However, as a commander of large forces in pitched battles he was not so competent, e.g. he made considerable mistakes at Naseby and Marston Moor. He gained a reputation for ruthlessness by slaughtering defenders at Bolton in 1644 and Leicester in 1645. In all, he is probably rather overrated.

Prince Rupert, commander of the Royalist cavalry.

commanders, especially Rupert. Some Royalist officers such as Lord George Goring were as interested in plunder as in winning battles.

MILITARY EVENTS OF THE FIRST CIVIL WAR 1642–6

The Battle of Edgehill, October 1642. The autumn of 1642 saw Charles advancing slowly on London with an army of about 10,000 men. The two sides met at Edgehill. The result was a draw, but the Parliamentary leader, the **Earl of Essex**, withdrew, leaving the way open to London. At this stage, a swift advance on London might have resulted in a Royalist victory, but the king, perhaps shaken by the first battle he had witnessed, moved too hesitantly, taking 'time out' to capture Oxford before advancing on London.

London 1642. In November 1642, Essex and his army made their way to London in front of the king. The Londoners turned out in their thousands and by the time Prince Rupert was burning Brentford, Essex had up to 24,000 men under his command, ready to defend the city at Turnham Green. Charles ignored Rupert's urgings to force the defences at Turnham Green and instead withdrew to Oxford. Not only did this ensure that the First Civil War would go on, but Charles had thrown away his best chance of a quick victory.

The war develops 1643. By the spring of 1643 most of the attempts at neutrality had broken down and several armies were in the field. The king's main field army was centred around Oxford, with Rupert commanding the cavalry. For Parliament, Essex remained in charge of the main field army, with the Eastern Association providing an army under the **Earl of Manchester**. The Parliamentary Western Army was under the command of Sir William Waller, while in Yorkshire the Fairfaxes, father and son, fought against the **Duke of Newcastle** from the clothing town strongholds of Leeds and Bradford.

The Royalist advance fails 1643. Charles may have planned a 'three-pronged' attack on the Parliament-held areas, designed to force his way to London, which he then intended to besiege into surrender. This presented the most serious threat to Parliament and made 1643 a crisis year for Pym. However, the strategy broke down during the course of the year.

The Duke of Newcastle decided to besiege Hull with his main forces rather than push further south and east. This decision seems to have been the result of some sharp checks that his forces had received from **Oliver Cromwell**'s newly trained cavalry. Newcastle also suffered from his supply lines becoming stretched and fears of an attack on his rear by the Hull garrison.

Charles decided to besiege Gloucester, the fall of which would have had a catastrophic effect on Parliamentary

KEY PEOPLE

The **Earl of Essex** was commander of the main field army of Parliament. He relieved Gloucester in 1643 and fought his way back to London. Essex had no authority over the other Parliamentary generals, but he has been blamed for Parliament's failure to win the war in 1643–4. He did make a very costly mistake in 1644: marching right down to Cornwall, he was defeated at Lostwithiel and 6,000 of his men were taken prisoner. His reputation never recovered. He was removed by the self-denying ordinance in 1645.

The **Earl of Manchester** commanded Parliament's Eastern Association Army. He was to fall out with Oliver Cromwell over his hesitant attitude to fighting to the finish, throwing away advantages that he had after Marston Moor and the second Battle of Newbury in 1644. Eventually, like Essex, he was removed from command by the self-denying ordinance.

The **first Marquis (later Duke) of Newcastle** was the commander of the king's Northern Army. Clarendon (who disliked him) wrote of him that he was 'as fit to be a General as a Bishop'. After the defeat at Marston Moor, in which his own regiment was slaughtered fighting to the last, he fled abroad and took no further part in the Civil War. His only abiding interest was the training of horses.

KEY PERSON

Oliver Cromwell rose to prominence as a cavalry commander in the Eastern Association. He promoted soldiers purely on merit, not on social background, and he insisted on iron discipline. By 1644 his 'Ironside' cavalry were the most important element in the Parliamentary armies.

A looting Civil War Soldier.

morale. Essex relieved Gloucester and, on his return march to London, found the king barring his path at Newbury on 20 September 1643. The first Battle of Newbury was a draw, but a strategic victory for Essex in that his forces were able to continue their march to London.

The contribution of Scots and Irish, autumn 1643. To win an advantage, both sides attempted to win allies from abroad:

- The king negotiated with the Irish rebels to allow him to bring 'English' regiments back from Ireland. However, the troops that did get back to England were captured by Sir William Brereton and promptly changed sides.
- Parliament negotiated help from the Scots. The Solemn League and Covenant between Parliament and the Scots was signed on September 1643. It meant that Newcastle's army coming south would be trapped between the Scots and the Eastern Association. The Scottish contribution was a significant contribution towards Parliamentary victory. Pym, who was the architect of the agreement, died in November 1643.

The fight for the north 1644. The Scots, under the Earl of Leven, crossed the border in January 1644. Newcastle's immediate problem was to prevent the Scots joining up with Fairfax's Hull troops. In April 1644 the commander of the Yorkshire Royalists, Lord Bellasis, was defeated at Selby, and Newcastle, who had moved north to face the Scots, was vulnerable to attack from the south. The Eastern Association Army was moving north to support Fairfax, and Newcastle retreated into York, caught in the vice. Prince Rupert rushed to his relief and actually managed to raise the Parliamentarian siege of York.

The Battle of Marston Moor, July 1644. Rupert then made an error. He offered battle at Marston Moor on 2 July 1644. The more sensible move would have been to gather all Newcastle's and his own forces and retreat, as Newcastle advised – his was, after all, the inferior force, perhaps 9,000 less than the Parliamentarians. But the real misjudgement was that, as it was drawing on towards evening, he assumed that there would be no battle that

Battles in Britain during the Civil Wars.

A print showing looting Cavaliers, published by supporters of Parliament during the Civil War.

day. The Parliamentarians, with Cromwell's cavalry in the lead, attacked and the king's Northern Army was destroyed. Significantly, the Eastern Association cavalry showed themselves to be a match for the Royalist horse.

Rupert managed to cut himself free with about 6,000 men, but the king had lost the north. The city of York surrendered within a fortnight. However, the opportunity to crush the other Royalist armies was not taken. The Scots went off to besiege Newcastle, Fairfax engaged in 'mopping up' operations against individual strongholds, while Manchester returned to the east. The failure of either side to win the war in 1643 was partly because neither side had a co-ordinated strategy.

The Creation of the New Model Army, winter 1644. These failures led to a reorganisation of the Parliamentary armies. In the winter of 1644, Essex and Manchester were sacked and the New Model Army of 22,000 men was created. The new army was placed under the command of Sir Thomas Fairfax, with Cromwell commanding the cavalry. The really reliable element was the old Eastern Association cavalry – the Ironsides – but gradually professionalism and discipline took hold in the infantry too.

There were two distinct features of the new army:

- **Promotion.** Its policy of promotion by merit was revolutionary and led to the rise of officers from humble backgrounds. However, the majority of the senior officers were, and remained in the future, from gentry families, e.g. Fairfax, Cromwell and Lambert.
- **Religious Independency.** Independency, hostile to both Anglicanism and Presbyterianism, spread rapidly, particularly in the ranks of the cavalry.

Naseby and its aftermath 1645. In June the king's main army was caught by the New Model Army at Naseby in Northamptonshire. Again, as at Marston Moor, the advantage in ground and numbers lay with the Parliamentarians, and again Rupert managed to smash the cavalry opposite him on the left. But, as usual, the Royalist cavalry did not wait for any further orders, but charged away to capture the Parliamentary luggage train. Rupert, a brilliant, dashing commander, had one dangerous fault: he never saw the importance of discipline *after* the first charge. Cromwell did. The Ironsides smashed the opposing Royalists on the right and then came to help the infantry in their battle with the Royalist infantry. The Royalists were completely destroyed and the king had lost his last field army capable of fighting a major pitched battle.

After that the New Model Army was fighting a series of 'mopping up' operations against smaller Royalist forces and laying drawn-out sieges of Royalist strongholds. In March 1646 the Royalist infantry surrendered at Stow-on-the-Wold. The king surrendered to the Scots in May and the last Royalist stronghold, Oxford, surrendered in June 1646.

Why did Parliament win the Civil War?

- Charles's strategic failures in 1642–3 when he still had some real chance of victory.
- Parliamentary control of the sea, which prevented arms/troops reaching the king from abroad.
- The Solemn League and Covenant – Scottish help in the north of England.
- The eventual creation of a central common structure and the New Model Army.

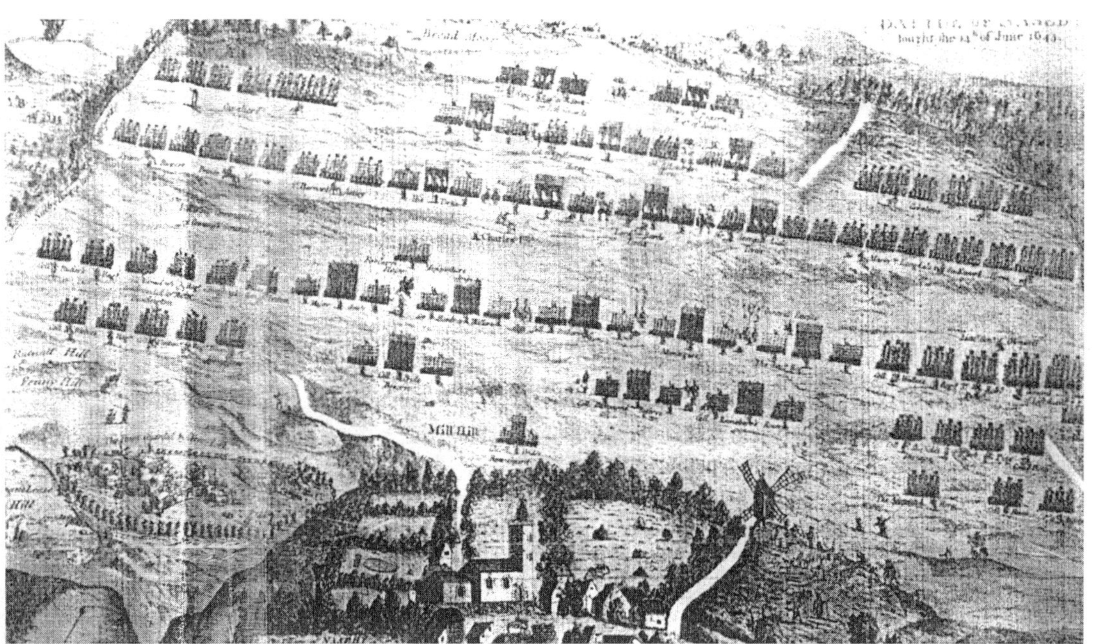

The battle of Naseby, 1645.

- Greater financial resources in the east and south of England.
- Possession of London and East Anglia – trade and wealth.
- Rather better organisation of the above financial resources: Pym.

THE POLITICAL HISTORY OF THE FIRST CIVIL WAR 1642–6

What were the three groupings in Parliament?

There were three loose groupings in Parliament. Their fortunes rose and fell as the Civil War progressed.

- **The Peace 'Party'.** The Peace Party was 'led' by Denzil Holles and was always hoping for a settlement. Most of them wanted only the end of the Anglican Church rather than further restrictions on the king's powers.
- **The Middle 'Party'.** The Middle Party always hoped that the king would 'see reason' and that a negotiated settlement could be found. They were the largest party and were led by Pym.

- **The War 'Party'.** Led by future republicans Sir Henry Vane and Sir Arthur Haselrige, the War Party tended to take a harder line on negotiations with the king. They believed that he would negotiate meaningfully only when defeated.

How did Parliament organise for war?

Finance. Parliament's finances were organised by Pym, who provided Parliament with enough money to fight the war. In February 1643 the assessments system was set up. Each county under Parliamentary control paid a tax, organised through County Committees. Compulsory loans were introduced in May 1643 and earlier, in April, fines were put upon Royalist supporters in Parliamentary areas and their estates were confiscated. They could regain them only by paying a heavy fine based on the value of the estate.

Manpower. In August 1643 Parliament accepted Pym's suggestion of an **impressment ordinance.** It was clear that the king was not willing to compromise. By 1645 at least half of Parliament's forces were people who were forced to fight.

Alliance with the Scots. In September 1643 Pym arranged a military alliance with the Presbyterian Scots. This was the Solemn League and Covenant. The Scots' price for military help was the establishment of a Presbyterian Church settlement in England after victory. Many MPs were less than enthusiastic about this prospect, but the king's negotiations with the Catholic Irish and the redeployment of royal troops from Ireland to England in September 1643 made an alliance with the Scots a priority.

Parliament after Pym. Pym died in December 1643. He had been the driving force behind Parliamentary opposition to the king since the Short Parliament of May 1640. He had then set up the machinery to win the war, and had held together the various shifting coalitions within Parliament. After his death the divisions re-emerged.

War and Peace parties. The split between the Peace Party and the War Party grew during 1644, while the Middle Party, the vast mass of MPs who had supported Pym,

KEY THEME

Pym's skill in holding the different parties together. These 'parties' were held together by Pym until his death in December 1643. His policy of attempting to negotiate with the king, while setting up the financial and administrative machinery to win the war, meant that MPs of all opinions could usually be persuaded to support his measures.

KEY TERM

An **impressment ordinance** enabled Parliament to conscript men to fight.

virtually ceased to exist. The majority of MPs moved towards the War Party's position. Parliament's leadership became increasingly divided on these lines.

- The Earl of Manchester was an intolerant hard-line Presbyterian inclined to the Peace Party, so his conduct of operations against the king was less than dynamic. He was fighting to bring the king to terms, not to defeat him.
- Cromwell, the cavalry commander, was the hero of the War Party. He seemed to be the one commander with the drive and military competence to win the war.

Religious issues. The division between Presbyterianism and Independents came to the fore in the autumn of 1644. Presbyterians were a clear majority in Parliament but Independent MPs were gaining in numbers and influence.

On 3 April 1645, MPs voted to remove Manchester, Essex and the other Parliamentary commanders by passing a 'self-denying ordinance'. This said that no member of either House of Parliament (apart from Oliver Cromwell) could hold a commission in the army. When the war finally ended in the summer of 1646, the War Party ceased to have any meaning. The king was beaten and, at the same time, threatening social, religious and political undercurrents were surfacing outside Westminster. So the basic conservatism of the majority of MPs reasserted itself; they expected, now the war was won, to be able to negotiate a settlement with the king.

Religious and political developments outside Parliament 1642–8

In many ways, the war created a much more complicated religious and political situation.

KEY THEME

Independents believed in religious toleration, i.e. that no one should be forced to attend church. They believed in 'self-governing' congregations that would choose their own minister.

Religious groups. The most important of these were as follows:

- **Independents.** A significant religious development was the growth in influence of Independency. Its ideas spread through the Parliamentary army from the cavalry of the Eastern Association, and its patron was Oliver

Cromwell. By 1646 Independency was challenging Parliamentary Presbyterianism.

- **The Sects.** Like Independents, they believed in a 'gathered church' of like-minded members, but rejected any idea of state church organisation.
- **Baptists.** These were the most numerous of the Sects. Often called Anabaptists, they believed in adult baptism, but were fairly conventional in their other religious ideas.
- **Fifth Monarchists.** They were convinced of the imminent coming of Christ, that there had been four monarchies in scripture and prophecy, and that the Fifth Monarchy would be the reign of 'King Jesus'.
- **Ranters and Muggletonians.** Some Sects, such as the Ranters and Muggletonians, had few members. They preached that 'sin was not sin unless the sinner thought it was'.

Political groups. The most important of these were as follows:

- **Clubmen.** In the increasing anarchy of the war, tired of looting troops, country people, in the west particularly, organised their districts into defensive pacts. Known as the Clubmen, they were determined to resist troops from either side entering their territory. These were farmers, cottagers and artisans practising self-help.
- **The Levellers.** The most important political development outside Parliament was the rise of the Levellers. Leveller ideas had first circulated in London, in pamphlet form. The main pamphleteers were **John Lilburne**, William Walwyn and Richard Overton. However, the Levellers were not a well-organised political party with a clear leadership structure. Their ideas, sometimes modified, had spread in London, but it was the army that was to be most influenced by, and influential in, Levellerism. The Levellers had influence out of all proportion to their numbers, but this was to be short-lived. The Levellers failed to force through the radical political programme that they put forward in the army debates at Putney in 1647 for the following reasons:

KEY THEME

Leveller ideas included:

- That in the state of nature, all men were naturally free and equal.
- That Englishmen were free in the past and had been enslaved by the Norman Conquest – 'the Norman Yoke'.
- That, as all were equal in the sight of God, so they should be in society.
- That the electoral system should be reformed so that there would be equal electoral districts.
- That all men over 21 should be able to vote.

KEY PERSON

John Lilburne was the most prominent Leveller. He joined the Parliamentary army, but left it in 1645 rather than sign the Covenant – the agreement to become a Presbyterian. Also in 1645 he published his first famous Leveller pamphlet – 'England's Birthright Justified' – which called for free speech and annual parliaments. He played some part in drawing up the Leveller programme of 1647, but he was an individualist not a leader of a political movement.

THE
World turn'd upside down:
OR,
A briefe description of the ridiculous Fashions
of these distracted Times.
By T.J. a well-willer to King, Parliament and Kingdom.
London: Printed for John Smith. 1647.

The front cover of a pamphlet called 'The World Turned Upside Down', published in about 1647.

- The majority of the army trusted Cromwell, rather than the Leveller spokesmen.
- The majority were interested more in bread-and-butter issues such as pay and indemnity than in paper constitutions.
- The Levellers, as already noted, had no clear leadership or organisational structure.
- Their most dynamic army representative, Colonel Rainborough, was killed in the Second Civil War.
- Cromwell put down the Leveller mutinies at Corkbush (1647) and Burford (1649) very rapidly before they could get out of hand.

THE SEARCH FOR A SETTLEMENT 1646–9

Introduction

From 1646 the gentry lost control of the situation. The result was that a series of events took place that shocked the traditional 'political nation'. These included the trial and execution of the king in 1649, the destruction of the old constitution with the abolition of the House of Lords and the establishment of a Republic – 'The Commonwealth of England'.

Charles' attitude

The role of Charles was crucial in explaining the events that followed the First Civil War. His attitude towards Parliament and his misunderstanding of his own situation had a crucial impact on the failure to reach a settlement. These were the main points of Charles' position:

- Far from seeing the logic of his position, he had no intention of giving up any of his powers and prerogatives.
- He saw himself as central to any agreement – he could not conceive a situation where he was not the key figure to be negotiated with and where his agreement would not be sought.
- As far as Charles was concerned, all his enemies – Parliament, the army, the Presbyterians, the Independents, the Scots – were traitors.
- Charles believed that any agreements could be broken and that his only duty was to regain his rightful God-given place as a divine right monarch. He played for time in negotiations, hoping that his enemies would fall out among themselves.

Parliament's attitude to peace

It was assumed by Parliament that Charles would now negotiate in good faith because he had been defeated. In these circumstances, leadership of the House of Commons passed to the opponents of the Independents in Parliament and of the army men. Their aims were:

- to come to an agreement with the king,

- to disband the hideously expensive and increasingly threatening army,
- to establish a national Presbyterian Church which all people would have to attend.

A typical believer in such ideas was Denzil Holles, the 'Peace Party' leader of 1642. By 1646 Holles was speaking and acting for the naturally conservative majority of the House of Commons. However, this programme was far too optimistic because it was based on several false beliefs. These were:

- that the army could be dispensed with, without paying its full arrears of pay,
- that the king would negotiate honestly with Parliament,
- that Independents both in the army and in a minority in Parliament could be suppressed or ignored.

The changed political situation

The beliefs held in 1642 among the 'moderate' gentry of Parliament were not so significant by 1646–7.

The attitude of the army. The army would not automatically obey Parliament. A significant majority had had their ideas fundamentally changed by the experience of soldiering in this unique army. Many soldiers had made the 'jump' from Independent thought in religion to independent political thought. By 1647 a minority of the New Model Army believed in radical political ideas. This was a force that had not existed in 1642 and a force without whose agreement no settlement could be reached.

Religious divisions. The Presbyterians hated Independency. To them Independents represented a potentially anarchical 'system' of Church government. Anglicanism was wrong, but so was the idea of the gathered congregation. Any agreement with Charles must include the establishment of the Presbyterian religion as the *state* religion, giving it the power to crush both Anglicans and the increasingly diffuse Independent congregations. Had Independency not had a power base in the army, perhaps this would have been a realistic aim. Independents were in the minority in the country and in Parliament, but the army gave them a strength that the Presbyterians in Parliament completely failed to grasp.

Relations between the army and Parliament. Many MPs, led by Denzil Holles, wanted to get rid of the army as soon as possible because they saw it as a threat to their position. The army wanted an Independent religious settlement and some of the army actually wanted to influence the negotiations with the king. Holles did not offer the army a reasonable financial settlement to encourage them to disband and go home. Therefore the army began to see that the only way to get what they believed were their rights was to interfere in any settlement with the king.

KEY ISSUE

The pay of the army. By 1647 the infantry were owed 18 weeks' pay; the cavalry 43 weeks'. Insultingly, Holles offered only 6 weeks' pay or service in Ireland. It was largely this treatment that caused the army to unite against Parliament.

'The Solemn Engagement'

The army, thoroughly disillusioned with Holles and the Presbyterian majority in Parliament, met at Newmarket on 29 May 1647, where 'The Solemn Engagement' was approved. The Engagement declared:

- The army would not disband until it had received a settlement that would have the approval of an Army Council.
- This Council would represent the opinions of all the army because it was to be composed of the general officers of the army, two commissioned officers from each regiment and two soldiers from each regiment.

The king's negotiations with Parliament

At Uxbridge in 1645 the king refused to accept a 'Presbyterian' settlement because the Royalist Montrose (later to be defeated) was still having successes for the Royalists in Scotland. On 5 May 1645, Charles surrendered to the Scots. While he was their prisoner, Charles received the **Newcastle Propositions** from Parliament. He played for time, but eventually accepted a modified form of the Propositions, or appeared to do so. This agreement could have opened up the prospect of a new coalition of forces against the army – a coalition of the Presbyterians in Parliament, the Royalists and the Scots. The Scots had entered the war on the side of Parliament in 1643 to ensure the victory of Presbyterianism, so they could now support the king against the Independent-

KEY EVENT

The Newcastle Propositions, July 1645.

- Presbyterianism was to be established in England.
- The Anglican Church and bishops were to be abolished.
- Presbyterianism would become the state religion that all had to accept.
- Parliament would have control over the armed forces for twenty years.

dominated army, which they feared and disliked as much as Holles and his Parliamentary colleagues did.

Denzil Holles.

Negotiations with the army

The army's reaction to this potential new alliance was to take steps to ensure that the army would be a main player in settlement negotiations with the king, while neutralising the potential threat that this coalition posed. Cornet Joyce with 500 troops went to Holdenby on 2 June, seized the king and brought him to the army at Newmarket. The army could now negotiate with the king directly. **'The Declaration of the Army'** followed.

KEY TERM

'The Declaration of the Army' stated the following:

- The army had been called 'to the defence of our own and the people's just rights and liberties'.
- Parliament should set a date for its own dissolution and be purged of the leading Presbyterian opponents of the army. Eleven Presbyterians withdrew.

So by June 1647 the chances of a slide into anarchy seemed higher. To all intents and purposes there were three different 'centres of authority', each claiming the right to decide a settlement – the king, Parliament and the army.

The army's offer to the king. The Army Council had put together the Heads of Proposals, and these were presented to Charles by Cromwell and Henry Ireton, the Commissary General. The king spun out the negotiations and ignored two important features of the Heads of Proposals:

- Parliamentary offers had all meant the destruction of the Anglican Church. Presbyterianism would become the state religion enforced by law; no other religions would be allowed. The Heads of Proposals, on the other hand, involved religious toleration, so by implication, the Church of England which Charles said he was defending could exist – but it would have no powers to make people attend its services.
- The army actually had the power to enforce a settlement whereas Parliament did not.

London 1647. On the 26 July 1647 a Presbyterian mob, possibly organised by Holles, invaded the House of Commons and the House of Lords. They attacked the Members of Parliament who wanted to come to an agreement with the army, restored the eleven Presbyterians who had withdrawn from Parliament and forced the Commons to pass a resolution inviting the king to come to

London. The leading 'Independent' members fled to the protection of the army. The response of the army was swift: it occupied London on 6 August, hoping to put some pressure on Parliament to 'see things their way' and accept the basic ideas of the 'Declaration' and the 'Heads'.

Army protest. By October 1647, a feeling of frustration in the army with Parliament and the king came to the surface when the army issued **'The Case of the Army Truly Stated'**. This was followed by remarkable debates in Putney Church, at which the Levellers in the army discussed with the senior officers what the future constitution of England should be. The representatives of each regiment – 'agitators' – were ranged against Cromwell and Ireton, whose more conservative political instincts would not allow them to consider such sweeping reforms as the Levellers put forward in the first **'Agreement of the People'**.

Views represented at the debates. The following views were represented:

- Cromwell opposed Leveller ideas on the grounds that they would lead to anarchy.
- Ireton argued against the Leveller idea of 'natural rights', and took the view that society was based upon property. Those without property could not be trusted to act responsibly because they had nothing to lose. Therefore, he argued that only those who had 'a permanent fixed interest in the Kingdom' should vote.
- One of the most radical of the Levellers, **Colonel Rainborough**, stood on the idea of 'natural rights', arguing that 'the poorest in England hath a life to lead as the greatest he' and that all should vote.

Failure to come to an agreement. The opposing views of the senior officers and the Levellers could not be reconciled, although Cromwell was anxious to keep the army together, fearing anarchy if it were to fall apart in arguments. He stressed what they all agreed on – some kind of reform and religious toleration. However, his sympathies on the subject of really radical political reforms were with Ireton and the other 'grandees', as the Levellers called the senior officers.

KEY TERMS

'The Case of the Army Truly Stated' demanded not only biennial parliaments (elections every two years), but that 'all free born Englishmen over 21 should vote' and that 'all power is originally . . . in the whole body of the people'.

'The Agreement of the People' demanded the following:

- biennial parliaments,
- no authority was above Parliament,
- nobody could be forced to do military service,
- all should be equal in the eyes of the law,
- parliamentary constituencies should be of the same size (this would get rid of many parliamentary seats that had only a few people voting and give more seats to areas where people were not so well represented),
- the present Parliament should be dissolved on 31 December 1648.

THE SECOND CIVIL WAR 1648

KEY PERSON

Colonel Thomas Rainborough. Originally a sailor, he fought in the army of the Eastern Association. A tough, ruthless soldier, he was the highest-ranking republican radical and the leading voice of the Levellers in the Putney debates. During the Second Civil War, he was murdered while unarmed. He was known to his supporters as 'the just, the valiant and the true'.

The Second Civil War was a series of uprisings, often with local grievances the driving force. Some Presbyterians joined the Royalists, but most remained neutral, as did the vast mass of the country, appalled by the prospect of another civil war.

Charles escapes. On 11 November 1647, Charles I escaped from army custody and allied himself with the Scots by the Engagement of 26 December. He also made contacts with English Royalists to organise risings. Parliament was, temporarily, as horrified by the implications of this as the army were and passed a 'Vote of No Addresses'; they would no longer negotiate with the king.

It was obvious that a second civil war was about to break out, with Charles, the Scots and Royalist elements ranged against the army and a very reluctant Parliament. In these circumstances, Leveller agitation died down. The main effect of Charles' actions was that Parliament and the army, grandees and radicals alike, united against Charles.

The Royalist cause collapses. Revolts in Kent, Essex, South Wales and Norwich were as much against high taxation, the hated county committees and the army as they were in favour of Charles. The risings were not well co-ordinated, nor did they attract the sort of mass support that would have made them victorious against the army. There was some vicious fighting, especially at Colchester, where executions took place after the fall of the town, but the army soon regained control. The Scottish invasion, perhaps the greatest threat, was halted by Cromwell in a brilliant action at Preston, where he inflicted a crushing defeat in August 1648. Charles himself had fled in November 1647 from Hampton Court to Carisbrooke Castle on the Isle of Wight. However, the governor of the castle, Robin Hammond (a cousin of Cromwell), imprisoned him.

THE TRIAL AND EXECUTION OF CHARLES I

Negotiations restart with the king. With the end of the Second Civil War, the gap between the 'conservative and moderate' largely Presbyterian majority in Parliament on one side, and a minority of Independent MPs and the army on the other, widened again.

The Presbyterian case. For the majority of MPs there could be no settlement without the king. Parliament could not accept the army's desire for religious toleration and radical political ideas, so a settlement with Charles was attractive, regardless of the past. Parliament would never agree to a trial of the king: such an action was simply unthinkable.

The army's decision to try the king. The army felt differently. It was largely united in the view that there could be no peace while Charles lived, and furious at the repeal of the 'Vote of No Addresses'. So it took the decision to try him. The army had to justify itself in the eyes of the world, so the trial of the king as a war criminal was essential, however dubious its legality. Some parliamentary element was needed to give the impression that the law was being observed – an army court martial would not do.

Pride's Purge 1648. On 6 December 1648, Colonel Pride, armed with a list of MPs whom the army was sure would never vote for a trial, stood at the door of the House of Commons. He kept out around 110 MPs, some being held in house arrest overnight. Another 250 MPs, seeing which way the wind was blowing, either withdrew or did not even attempt to enter. This left 60 or so members who would agree to a trial.

Charles' conduct at the trial. Throughout Charles' trial he refused to plead or speak on the legal grounds that there was no law that could try him. It is possible that Charles saw the trial as a bluff to try to force him into a settlement. After Bradshaw, the presiding judge, passed the sentence of death, Charles suddenly tried to speak for the first time, as if he finally realised that the trial was in earnest. On

KEY THEMES

The reaction of the army to the Second Civil War. The Presbyterian majority in Parliament would never harm the king personally, but at the Windsor prayer meeting, held before the army went off to fight in March 1648, they swore to bring 'that man of blood, Charles Stuart, to an account for the blood that he had shed'.

Cromwell's attitude to the trial. Characteristically, Cromwell, who was engaged in a 'mopping up' operation against Pontefract Castle when Pride's Purge occurred, seems to have been in two minds about the advisability of a trial. But once his mind was made up, he went through with it. The Dutch envoys who came to plead for Charles' life were told by Cromwell, 'We will cut off his head with the crown on it.'

A painting showing the execution of Charles I in 1649.

30 January 1649, Charles passed to the scaffold through the Banqueting Hall in Whitehall. His dignity on the scaffold impressed many and created the legend of the 'royal martyr' that was to haunt the Republic that followed.

AS ASSESSMENTS

ENGLAND 1603–29

Sources exercises in the style of AQA

1 Study the sources below and then answer the questions.

Source A

First, as in all Parliaments, it is the king's office to . . . make good laws. The main reason why this Parliament is called . . . is for to sustain me in my urgent financial necessity . . . The next cause of calling this Parliament . . . is the miserable spectacle of the Palatinate invaded . . . But I can do nothing without sustenance from my people, and never king of England had less supply [money] than I have had . . . But you of the Lower House, I would not have you to meddle with the complaints against the king, the Church or state matters, nor with princes' prerogatives. The Parliament was never called for that purpose. And if among you there be such a busy body, he is the spirit of Satan that means to overthrow the good errand in hand.

Adapted from James I's speech to Parliament, 30 January 1621.

Source B

The Commons make this protestation . . . That the privileges of Parliament are the ancient and undoubted birthright and inheritance of the subjects of England: and that the . . . affairs concerning the king, state and defence of the realm and of the Church of England, and the maintenance and making of the laws, and redress of grievances . . . are proper subjects and matters of counsel and debate in Parliament.

Adapted from the Commons' Protestation, 18 December 1621.

Source C

James' personal relations with Parliament did not a little to put the Commons on the offensive. His want of dignity in carriage was no greater handicap to him than his want of dignity in political conduct. Elizabeth had held herself in the background, appearing at the beginning and the end of sessions, occasionally sending a message . . . His itch for meddling and utterance made it impossible for him to remain in the background . . . Royal words lost their weight . . . few kings have been so fitted by nature to call forth an Opposition and put government on the defensive.

Adapted from 'The Winning of the Initiative by the House of Commons', by Wallace Notestein, British Academy Lecture, 1924. (It could be noted that many historians now agree with Notestein.)

Questions

Reading. Before answering these questions, you should have read pages 25–53 of this book.

1 Study Source A. Explain the meaning of the term 'princes' prerogatives' in the context of James I and his parliaments. Use your own knowledge to answer this question.

How to answer this question. There are usually only three marks for this type of question, so do not spend too much time on it in an examination.

- You should show that you are aware of the areas of 'princes' prerogatives', e.g. foreign policy and command of the armed forces.
- The question also asks you to show an understanding of 'the context' of James I and his parliaments. In your answer, therefore, you should explain the prerogatives at issue during James' parliaments, e.g. disputed elections.

2 Study Source B. Explain how useful this source is to the historian studying parliamentary privilege in 1621.

How to answer this question. In answering this question, you need to address the following points:

- Top-quality answers will discuss both the positive value and the limitations of the source.
- Compare the source's positive points and its limitations and also consider its reliability. You must also compare the usefulness of the source against your own knowledge.
- You are also expected to mention the extent to which the author's views are typical of the period. Another question you should ask is: what gaps are there in the evidence?
- The usefulness of a source depends on the questions asked of it. An example of such a question might be: can it be corroborated (backed up) with other evidence?

Style. To reach the top level, you should try to structure your answer so as to look at the positive points and the limitations of the source. Below is an extract from an answer to this question, which looks at the limitations of the source.

This source is useful to a historian in that it reflects Parliament's concern at the attitude of James. It reflects the tension between Crown and Parliament over their rights and the belief that Parliament had the right to be consulted. It is particularly useful because the Commons' Protestation shows the view of the majority of the Commons, and protestations of this type were rare.

3 Study Sources A, B and C. You should also use your own knowledge to answer this question. To what extent was James I the cause of the problems he faced in his relations with Parliament between 1621 and 1624?

How to answer this question. To answer this type of question, you must do the following:

- **Analyse.** As has been suggested above, you must analyse throughout your response to the question.
- **Evidence.** Your line of argument must be backed up with accurate information. You should also show an understanding of the demands of the question by selecting material from the sources and your own knowledge.
- **Balance.** Cover all the parts of the question with reasonable balance.
- **Attempt to offer judgement.** This might be in the conclusion, but you should try to make judgements throughout your answer.
- **Structure.** You must try to structure your responses into paragraphs. You will also be judged on the quality of your written English.

Plan. Before you write an answer to this question, it is important that you write a plan. Your plan should include the main points of argument or analysis that you are going to use to answer the question. Examples of your main points in writing this essay are as follows:

- James was responsible to the extent that he provoked concern in Parliament because he appeared on occasions not to understand Parliament's rights.
- Tension developed partly because James had come from Scotland, where the role of the Scottish Parliament was very different, and partly because James did stress in his speeches the 'divine' nature of monarchy.
- However, James should not carry all the blame. His problems arose in part because of parliaments wishing to assert their rights in a way that they hadn't done in the last years of Elizabeth.

Using sources. The following information from the sources can be used:

- **Source A** has a demanding tone, which was bound to provoke Parliament. James attacks those in Parliament who might 'meddle' and equates dissent with treachery. The evidence in this source points to James' attitude being a key factor in increasing tension between Crown and Parliament.
- **Source B** shows how Parliament was upset by James' attitude. You might point out how Parliament felt it necessary to define its areas of discussion.
- **Source C** gives the candidate the chance to compare the attitude of Parliament towards Elizabeth and James. You might choose to quote from the source, e.g. 'few kings have been so fitted by nature to call forth an Opposition'.

Using own knowledge. You can use your own knowledge from reading Chapters 1 and 2 of the book. The main themes you should refer to are:

- the significance of the Spanish marriage scheme and the war in Europe – these were vital in causing problems between Parliament and the king;
- the issue of favourites, especially Buckingham, and the unpopularity of the Earl of Middlesex;
- economic problems and the unpopularity of monopolies;
- religious issues.

Style. Here is an example of a direct style using evidence.

One should not exaggerate James' difficulties with Parliament. Certainly there were problems with James' foreign policy, as referred to in Source A: 'the miserable spectre of the Palatinate invaded'. But as James points out in Source A, Parliament did not provide him with sufficient funds to intervene militarily in the Palatinate. The 1621 parliament broke up without money being voted. Therefore the responsibility for the problems should be placed as much with the Commons as with James. However, in 1621 James was not considering war with Spain in any case.

2 Read Source A and then answer the questions.

Source A

But in the truth the king had done great harm . . . He had first encouraged Puritans, then called them to argue a case already decided against them and treated them with scorn. From now on conformity was to be more rigidly enforced; and the Church was to become more narrow.

Adapted from *King James VI and I*, by D. H. Willson, 1956, on the subject of the Hampton Court Conference.

1 Explain the meaning of the Puritan 'case' as mentioned in the source.

How to answer this question. The question wants you to focus your answer on the Puritan case as mentioned in Source A. You should try to explain the Puritans' call for reform of Church administration and Church ceremonies, much of this being explained in the Millenary Petition.

Style. You need to answer the question directly. Here is an example of a sentence showing how you might do that.

> *The Puritan case was expressed in a number of petitions presented to the king in 1603–4, an example being the Millenary Petition of 1603. Central to the Puritan case was the demand for the changes in Church administration, most noticeably the removal of bishops.*

2 Why did James want religious conformity?

How to answer this question. Although there is a source at the start of the exercise, the question does not ask you to use it if you do not want to. Instead the source can act as a stimulus, giving you a clue to at least a part of your answer. In this case, it mentions the increasing scorn with which James treated the Puritans.

The question here wants you to explain the main reasons why James wanted to impose conformity. To reach the top level, you should prioritise the factors you give. These factors might be: protection of the political and social order, 'no bishop, no king', protection of the royal prerogative and control of the localities.

Plan. Before you start, you should briefly plan your answer. Because this is a seven-mark question, you should not spend too much time planning. Below is an example of a key point that you might put in your plan:

- James wished for conformity primarily because any potential changes to the Church might well undermine royal authority.

3 How successful was James I in his attempts to achieve religious conformity?

How to answer this question. For this question, the source should be used only as a stimulus. The question asks for an analytical answer. Therefore you need to do the following:

- Answer with a strong line of argument and make a clear judgement that comes down on one side or the other of the question.
- Show that you understand that James was more successful in some areas than others.
- Use well-selected evidence to back up your argument.

Plan. Before you start writing, you should plan your answer. This plan should start with the key points of argument that you will explain throughout your answer. Below are some key points that you could use.

- James was successful in that he was prepared to be flexible but was not prepared to accept 'extreme' demands, as shown at the Hampton Court Conference.
- James' idea of conformity was broad, so most people were prepared to accept the Church of England as James saw it. Therefore he was fundamentally successful.
- It is hard to see how all Protestants could accept any state church.

Content. You might refer in your answer to James' policies towards different groups: Catholics, Arminians, Puritans, the Scottish Church. You should refer to specific detail, e.g. Millenary Petition, Hampton Court, appointment and attitude of Abbott or the Recusancy Laws.

3 Read Source A and then answer the questions.

Source A

I cannot but confess that it is in an horror to think upon . . . the greatness of my debts and the smallness of my means. It is true my heart is greater than my rent, and care to preserve my honour . . . by payment of my debts far greater than my possibility.

Adapted from a letter from James I to Robert Cecil, 1604, quoted in *James I, King of Great Britain*, by Irene Carrier.

1 What does James mean by 'the greatness of my debts and the smallness of my means'? Use the source and your own knowledge to answer this question.

How to answer this question. The question is asking you to give a detailed explanation of the quote, using the source and your own knowledge. When referring to the information from the source, you should use short quotes where appropriate.

Using the source. In the source there are references to James' generosity – 'my heart is greater than my rent' – and to the fact that he has insufficient funds for the 'payment of my debts'.

Using own knowledge. From your own knowledge, you could explain that James had significant financial problems due to his extravagance and the nature of royal income. There were also real problems in introducing financial reform.

Style. There will usually be a maximum of three marks for this type of question, so you must try to be as concise as possible. Here is an example of a sentence in response to this question.

The debts to which James refers were mainly the result of his expenditure. On assuming the throne of a significantly wealthier country, James spent extravagantly.

2 Explain how successive attempts were made to improve James' financial situation in the period 1603–25.

How to answer this question. This question asks for a straightforward explanation. You should be aware of the need to explain the various attempts at reform within the context of a key theme. It is important that you use a wide range of accurate evidence in your answer.

Plan. A key theme that you might use is that the attempts at reform were numerous. However, they failed to meet the problem of balancing the Crown's finances because of James' extravagance and the increase in the costs of government.

Content. Your answer might include an explanation of the Great Contract, the work of Cranfield, impositions, monopolies, wardship and court fines.

3 To what extent was James responsible for his own financial problems?

How to answer this question. The question asks for an analytical answer. Therefore you need to do the following:

- Answer with a strong line of argument, and make a clear judgement that comes down on one side or the other of the question.
- Show that you understand that James was more successful in some areas than others.
- Use well-selected evidence to back up your argument.
- You need to work out clearly in your mind what you think is the most important reason for James' financial problems. In your answer, you should give a balanced explanation which shows the links between James' extravagance and problems of Crown income and the cost of government.

Plan. You must identify your main points of argument. Below are examples of the points you might make:

- The Crown was not in a strong financial position in 1603. Inflation and the sale of Crown lands had already damaged revenue.

- Subsidies were under-assessed and therefore caused the Crown significant loss of revenue.
- However, James was extravagant and none of his ministers was able to curb his spending effectively.

Sources exercise in the style of Edexcel

4 Study Source A and then answer the questions.

Source A

He was guided more by the rules of appetite than of judgement and exalted almost all of his own family and dependants, people who had no virtue or merit other than their alliance with him. This offended both the ancient nobility and people of all conditions. The revenues of the Crown were sacrificed to the enriching of a private family. Buckingham was fearless; his loyalty to his friends was vehement, but he was an unforgiving enemy; he was impetuous. His ascent was so quick that it seemed rather a flight than a growth. He was in his nature just and candid, liberal, generous and bountiful. If he had huge ambition, with which he was accused, it was as a weed which grew in the best soil. It was no more in his power to be without promotion, and titles and wealth, than for a healthy man to sit in the sun and remain without any warmth.

Adapted from 'Observations on the Duke of Buckingham in the 1620s' written by Edward Hyde, Earl of Clarendon. The 'Observations' were published in his *History of the Rebellion* in 1702.

1 Using the source, explain why Buckingham was so hated in England in the 1620s.

How to answer this question. The question wants you to focus your answer on Source A.

- In asking you to explain your answer, the question is also hoping that you will be able to draw out some of the less obvious points from the source, e.g. that Buckingham's rapid rise caused jealousy among the established courtiers.
- You should quote from the source whenever possible. However, you should ensure that your quotes are short and to the point.

Style. You need to answer the question directly. Here is an example of a sentence showing how you might do that.

The most important reason why Buckingham was hated is that he showed little judgement and promoted his clients and family. This is shown in the source where Clarendon complains of this offending 'the ancient nobility'.

2 Why did England go to war against Spain in 1624–5?

How to answer this question. Although there is a source at the start of the exercise, the question does not ask you to use it if you do not want to. Instead the source can act as a stimulus.

The question wants you to analyse the reasons why England went to war against Spain in the 1620s. You should mention the following points:

- Pressure for England to go to war stemmed from the European context.
- There was also pressure from influential individuals/groups in England, e.g. Buckingham and Charles after the Spanish marriage episode.

3 Why did Charles I have a bad relationship with Parliament in the years 1625–9?

How to answer this question. For this question you are to use the source, but only as a stimulus. The question asks for an analytical answer, therefore you need to do the following:

- Answer with a strong line of argument and make a clear judgement that comes down on one side or the other of the question.
- Show that you understand that various groups within society saw their lives improve, but for some their lives worsened.
- Use well-selected evidence to back up your argument.

Plan. To answer this question you need to plan first. Your plan should include clear points of argument that you can follow through in your answer. Here are some examples of key points of argument.

- Most importantly, Charles' strong belief in divine right and his inability to explain his actions made Parliament suspicious.
- His promotion of High Church Arminians offended many, as did his relationship with Buckingham.
- Equally important was the failure of his and Buckingham's foreign policy during this period.
- He appeared to ignore the rights of his subjects and this led to the Petition of Right of 1628.

Style. Your style needs to be analytical and to the point. Here is an example of a couple of sentences from an answer to the question. Note how the candidate is direct in her response. She is discussing the last point in the plan.

By 1628 martial law and the imprisonment of those who refused to pay forced loans had created a fear in Parliament that Charles was prepared to bend the law and ignore the rights of his subjects. This created considerable tension, resulting in the Petition of Right.

Essay in the style of Edexcel

Reading. To answer this question you need to read pages 16–33.

1 Explain why Puritanism was such an important issue for James I from 1603 to 1610.

How to answer this question. The question asks you to analyse the challenge posed by Puritanism in the first seven years of James' reign. The emphasis of the essay is on the importance of Puritanism as an issue, and you need to produce an argument that focuses on this specifically.

Plan. You need to plan your essay to avoid simply running through a narrative account of the development of Puritanism. You need, in particular, to identify the points of argument that would allow you to do this. Here are some examples:

- The importance of the development of Puritanism was that discussion of the Church went to the heart of the issue of royal prerogative and the role of James I as king.
- The Puritans posed an important challenge in James' early years. Their proposals, such as those presented at Hampton Court, threatened to undermine his credibility and position.

Content. You must ensure that the content of your answer covers the whole period in question. Those who focus only on an important event such as the Hampton Court Conference stand to be penalised. You should make reference to the following in your essay:

- the nature of the Church of England and the criticisms of it made by the Puritans;
- puritan petitions, including the Millenary Petition of 1603;
- the issue of the bishops and James' stance on the subject;
- the Hampton Court Conference;
- Bancroft's canons;
- Puritan attitudes to James' foreign policy.

THE ENGLISH CIVIL WAR 1637–49

Sources exercise in the style of OCR

1 Read the sources and then answer the questions.

Source A

The restraint of many godly and able men from the ministry and the thrusting out from many congregations of their faithful and diligent ministers.

The publishing of Popish, Arminian and other dangerous books and teachings, as namely, 'That the Church of Rome is a true Church and in the worst times never erred in fundamentals'; 'that the subjects have no property in their estates but that the King may take from them what he pleaseth'.

The growth of Popery.

The present wars and commotions between His Majesty and his subjects of Scotland.

Grievances against the bishops listed in the Root and Branch Petition, presented by 15,000 citizens of London in December 1640.

Source B

There is no man within these walls more sensible of the heavy grievances of Church government than myself, nor whose affections are keener to the clipping of the wings of the bishops. But having reason to believe that some aim at a total abolition of bishops, which is against my heart, I cannot restrain myself from labouring to divert this petition. I do not think a king can totally put down bishops with safety to monarchy. Let us resolve upon a thorough reformation, but let us not destroy bishops but make them such as they were in the primitive times.

Sir George Digby, MP, speaking against the Root and Branch Petition in the House of Commons, 9 February 1641.

Source C

As for depriving the bishops of their votes in Parliament, we would have you consider that their right is grounded upon the fundamental law of the kingdom and the constitution of Parliament . . . But we are persuaded in our conscience that no Church can be found upon earth that professes the true religion with more purity of doctrine than the Church of England which, by the grace of God, we will with constancy maintain not only against all invasions of Popery but also from the irreverence of schismatics and separatists.

The King's answer to the petition accompanying the Grand Remonstrance, 23 December 1641.

1 What is meant by 'the present wars and commotions'? Use Source A and your own knowledge to answer this question.

How to answer this question. The question asks you to focus on the quote and explain its meaning in detail. To reach the highest mark, you must make sure that you explain the quote in detail and relate it to the Root and Branch Petition.

Content. These are the suggested areas for discussion in your answer:

- The phrase refers to the war against the Scottish Presbyterian rebels. You should explain that this was triggered by Archbishop Laud's attempt to force a High Church Prayer Book on Scotland in 1637.
- Many English Puritans had sympathy for the Scots and applauded their attack on the bishops.
- The Root and Branch Petition of 1641 was an attempt to remove bishops in England because for Puritans they were seen as part of the Laudian attempt to push the Church of England in a Catholic direction.

2 Study Source C and explain how useful it is as evidence about Charles' attitude to the Church and his position as head of the Church of England.

How to answer this question. This question is about the usefulness of the source. Before answering this question you should consider the following points:

- Top-quality answers will discuss both the positive value and the limitations of the source.
- Compare its positive points and limitations, and also consider its reliability. You must also compare the usefulness of the source against your own knowledge.
- You are also expected to mention the extent to which the author's views were typical of the period. Another question you should ask is: what gaps are there in the evidence?
- The usefulness of a source depends on the questions asked of it. An example of such a question might be: can it be corroborated (backed up) with other evidence?

3 Study Sources A and B. Compare the views of these two sources in their attitudes towards the bishops.

How to answer this question. To gain top marks you need to compare these two sources, pointing out the areas of agreement and disagreement. There should be a balance for the top mark.

Content. You might wish to comment on and explain the following points more fully:

- The sources agree in that there are problems with the bishops.
- Source B differs from Source A in that it is opposed to the abolition of the bishops, merely wishing to return the bishops to their original role as spiritual leaders. This opposes Laud's view that bishops should have wide-ranging political and legal powers.
- Source B makes the point that bishops are part of the system of monarchy. This is not considered in Source A.

4 How far do you agree with the view that 'Defence of the Church of England was the main reason for a reaction in favour of Charles I by late 1641.' Use all the sources and your own knowledge to answer this question.

How to answer this question. You should do the following:

- Sustain an argument and draw conclusions using the sources and, importantly, your own knowledge.
- Interpret the meaning of the sources in the light of the question.
- Show that you understand the question by making a clear judgement, perhaps in the conclusion.
- Prioritise the factors that you are discussing.
- The evaluation and interpretation of each source does not have to be lengthy. You must refer to the sources, however, and you must use you own knowledge to inform your judgement. Again, your own knowledge does not have to be written out at any great length.
- Make a judgement about the sources' utility and reliability given what they say and how that compares with what you know. You must also judge the authors of the sources and their situation and motives against what you know.

Plan. You should plan your answer thoroughly before you start.

Style. Below is an example of how you might answer this question. Note that the candidate interprets the source, uses his own knowledge and evaluates the source as evidence.

Many MPs in November 1640 were deeply concerned about the way that Laudian bishops appeared to be pushing the Church towards Roman Catholicism. They also deeply resented Church courts and the powers of the bishops that Laud had tried to reinstate. As shown in Source A, some people took the view that the whole idea of bishops was corrupt and associated with Roman Catholicism. Therefore the bishops had to be abolished. Others took the view, as shown in Source B, that bishops had to return to their original 'primitive origins' and then the Church of England would be acceptable. These people took the view that the old Elizabethan bishops as opposed to the new Laudian bishops were part of the social structure and a vital part of the

Church. However, Source A can been seen as unrepresentative in the sense that it is a result of stirring up the more extreme London Puritans, whose views would probably not be those of the majority. Source B shows an attempt to win over the moderates in Parliament. However, Sir George Digby was not himself a moderate and became a Catholic covert.

Essays in the style of Edexcel

1 Describe the role of Archbishop Laud during the period 1629–40.

How to answer this question. In this type of question, you need to do the following:

- Write a detailed explanation in response to the question.
- Use well-selected evidence. The material you use must be directly relevant to the question, and accurate.
- Cover the relevant areas as demanded by the question.
- Organise your work into clear paragraphs.

Plan. You need to plan your answer very carefully. It would be best for you to break your answer up into different themes. These should include:

- the beauty of holiness – Laud's desire to change the Church's ceremonies and the appearance of the parish church;
- Laud's determination to raise the status of the bishops and the parish clergy;
- Laud's desire to reassert the legal rights of the Church;
- Laud's support for divine right monarchy.

Style. Below is an extract from an answer to this question.

Laud objected to the idea that bishops and the parish clergy should defer to the gentry. He insisted that the clergy stood up to the local gentry and, in some cases, where the gentry found themselves in disagreement with the Church he brought them to Church courts. He insisted in the 1630s that private pews were removed and that the gentry respected their local minister.

2 Why, by 1640, had Personal Rule collapsed?

How to answer this question. In this question you need to do the following:

- Sustain an argument throughout your answer.
- Support your argument with selected information.
- Prioritise the relative importance of the factors.
- Organise your answer into paragraphs.

Plan. Before you answer this question, you must complete a comprehensive and thorough plan. Below are examples of the key points you might make.

- War with Scotland meant that Charles was effectively bankrupt and had to call Parliament.
- This war was not popular with the English, who saw the Scots as suffering from the same Laudian oppressions as they were. As a result, they did not fight effectively, thus leading to Charles' defeat and the end of Personal Rule.
- Charles had not followed popular policies in the 1630s and there was great suspicion of a Catholic conspiracy.
- Charles had destroyed his credit with the merchants of the City of London, and so he could not borrow to fight a war.
- In these circumstances, humiliatingly defeated and with the Scots occupying the six northern counties and being paid £850 a day not to advance further south, Charles had no choice but to call Parliament.

Style. Below is an extract from an answer to this question.

The fall of Personal Rule was not the result of a revolt by the gentry, however unpopular Charles' policies, financial and religious, were. The fall of Personal Rule that forced Charles to call Parliament in 1640 was directly caused by the Scottish wars. Laud's and Charles' disastrous policy of trying to force a 'High Church' prayer book on the strongly puritan Scots in 1637 led to a revolt of his Scottish subjects. This was a revolt that, despite previous dislike between the English gentry and the Scots, found some sympathy amongst the 'puritan' English gentry. The ineffectiveness of English forces against the Scots was not just a question of an inefficient militia, ill equipped and ill trained, but a reluctance to fight 'fellow sufferers' of Laud's policies. Thus some troops, raised to fight the Scots, hanged their Roman Catholic officers and smashed down altar rails in churches, before deserting at the first opportunity. The end result was that Charles was forced to call Parliament in order to raise money to pay the Scots not to continue to advance.

INDEX